Explode The Code® 2nd Edition

Teacher's Guide for Books 1 and 2

Nancy Hall

EDUCATORS PUBLISHING SERVICE
Cambridge and Toronto

Printed in Benton Harbor, MI, in May 2019
ISBN 978-0-8388-7822-4

6 7 8 9 10 PPG 23 22 21 20 19

Introduction

Explode The Code (ETC) provides a time-tested approach to teaching phonics. *ETC* breaks down the learning of phonic elements into manageable chunks so that children continually feel success as they move through the program.

Based on the Orton-Gillingham technique, *ETC* is equally suitable for one-on-one instruction and group or whole-class instruction. A clearly established routine helps provide students with a "road map" through each lesson, so learning a new set of instructions never interferes with learning new skills. The instruction is straightforward and sensible. (See Lesson Routine at a Glance on the inside front cover.) *Explode The Code* is designed to be used with other ELA materials, such as literature and decodable readers. For a variety of appropriate EPS decodable readers, both print and eBooks, see eps.schoolspecialty.com/products/literacy/decodable-readers.

Systematic, Direct Teaching of Phonics

Jeanne Chall's *Learning to Read: The Great Debate*—an extensive review of classroom, laboratory, and clinical research—revealed the efficacy of a direct, explicit, systematic teaching of decoding skills. Chall concluded that code emphasis programs produced better results, "not only in terms of the mechanical aspects of literacy alone, as was once supposed, but also in terms of the ultimate goals of reading instruction—comprehension and possibly even speed of reading" (Chall 1967, 307).

Even as new understandings about learning and teaching have evolved in the years since 1967, these findings have been repeatedly reconfirmed (Bond and Dykstra 1967; Chall 1983; Adams 1990; National Reading Panel 2000). In 2000, the National Reading Panel presented its findings of studies published since 1970, comparing phonics instruction with other kinds of instruction. Focusing on kindergarten through sixth grade, the panel concluded that systematic phonics instruction enhanced children's ability to read, spell, and comprehend text, particularly in the younger grades. These results were especially evident in the word-reading skills of disabled readers and children from low socioeconomic backgrounds, and in the spelling skills of good readers.

Chall and Popp write of "two kinds of meaning—meaning of the medium (the print) and the meaning of the message (the ideas)" (1996, 2). Knowledge of phonics gives students the ability to decode print, which in turn reveals the message ideas. The more words early readers can recognize, the more

accessible meaning becomes. Children who have difficulty identifying words lack the fluency needed to concentrate on meaning (Rasinsky 2000). Conversely, children who are given direct, systematic instruction in decoding skills have the tools for developing fluent, meaningful reading. Furthermore, they have the tools to produce print and consequently express their thoughts in writing, which in turn reinforces their word identification skills (Ehri, 1998).

While the place of direct, systematic phonics in the teaching of reading has changed throughout the years, one thing has always been true: Children need to "break the code"—the sound-symbol correlation—in order to decode and comprehend what they read. And while a small percentage of children can do this partly or mostly on their own, the overwhelming majority of children need direct instruction, with some needing intervention and more practice.

Explode The Code offers a complete systematic phonics program for the elementary grades. Phonetic elements and patterns, carefully sequenced to consider both frequency of use and difficulty, are presented in sequence and practiced in a series of instructive workbooks. Teacher's Guides accompany all the books.

The recent Common Core State Standards initiative has been a controversial one, but the section known as the "Foundational Skills" is perhaps the least controversial, as it merely restates the need for skills students have long been known to require in order to be successful readers: For example, the Foundational Skills say:

"These standards are directed toward fostering students' understanding and working knowledge of concepts of print, the alphabetic principle, and other basic conventions of the English writing system. These foundational skills are not an end in and of themselves; rather, they are necessary and important components of an effective, comprehensive reading program designed to develop proficient readers with the capacity to comprehend texts across a range of types and disciplines. [emphasis ours] *Instruction should be differentiated: good readers will need much less practice with these concepts than struggling readers will."*
(CCSSI, 15)

The CCSS go on to provide signposts along the way to literacy that differ little from the Scope and Sequences of skills provided within most any phonics program.

The first three books of the *Explode The Code* series—Books A, B, and C—focus on visual identification of consonants, their written lowercase forms, and their sound–symbol relationships. An engaging, colorful wall chart with felt objects representing key words for the twenty-six letters of the alphabet may be used to introduce children to the names and sounds of the lowercase letters and/or to reinforce lessons in books A, B, and C. An activity book with instructions for thirty-five games comes with the wall chart. Key word picture–letter cards are also available for Books A, B, and C, while Code Cards reinforce and review the letter sounds taught in Books 1–3 ½.

The remaining eight books—*Explode The Code* Books 1–8—progress through the vowel sounds and patterns, consonant clusters and digraphs, syllables, and suffixes. A pretest at the beginning of Book 1 helps teachers ensure that students are ready for work with these phonic elements. Posttests are found at the end of each workbook. If these show that extra practice is needed, additional workbooks, from 1 ½ to 6 ½, provide this extra practice in the same skills as the matching whole number book. Posttests at the end of these "half" books will ensure that children are ready to progress to the next level. A separate criterion-referenced Placement Test is available to assess the specific phonic concepts children know and those they need to be taught.

Through systematic direct teaching of phonics using *Explode The Code*, the following successes in reading and writing occur:

- The alphabetic principle is firmly established.
- Phonological awareness skills are fostered alongside the phonics teaching.
- Understanding of how sound–symbol relationships permit words and text to be decoded and encoded is fully developed and practiced, enhancing fluency and automaticity.
- Students of varying language and skill needs are accommodated through vocabulary and concept building, exposure to differing approaches to teaching phonics, and flexible grouping and use of the materials.
- See more about the research for this series at http://epsbooks.com.

References

Adams, M.J. (1990). Beginning to Read: Thinking and Learning about Print. Cambridge, MA: MIT Press.

Bond, G. & Dykstra, R. (1967). "The cooperative research program in first grade reading." Reading Research Quarterly 2: 5–142.

Chall, J.S. (1967, 1983). Learning to Read: The Great Debate. New York: McGraw-Hill.

Chall, J.S. & Popp, H.M. (1996). Teaching and Assessing Phonics, Why, What, When, How: A Guide for Teachers. Cambridge, MA: Educators Publishing Service.

Common Core State Standards Initiative. (2010) Common Core State Standards for English Language Arts & Literacy in History/Social Studies, Science, and Technical Subjects. Washington, DC, National Governors Association Center for Best Practices and the Council of Chief State School Officers.

Ehri, L.C. (1998). "Grapheme–phoneme knowledge is essential for learning to read words in English." In: Metsala, J.L. & Ehri, L.C. (eds.) Word Recognition in Beginning Literacy. Mahway, NJ: Erlbaum, 3–40.

National Reading Panel (2000). Teaching Children to Read: An Evidence Based Assessment of the Scientific Research Literature on Reading and Its Implication for Reading Instruction: Reports of the Subgroups. Washington: National Institute of Child Health and Development.

Rasinsky, T.V. (2000). "Does speed matter in reading?" The Reading Teacher 54:146–151.

Explode The Code Books A–C Teacher's Guide

Explode The Code Teacher's Guides expand on the skills presented in the student books, providing teachers with various options for instruction and reinforcement. The guides address the principles of phonemic awareness, phonics, vocabulary, fluency, and comprehension as they relate to each new skill presented in the lesson. They also include suggestions for writing practice and reinforcement. Each lesson follows the same easy-to-use format:

Materials and Picture Book Suggestions   Each lesson provides a list of coordinating *Explode The Code* Wall Chart and Picture–Letter Card materials that may be used during instruction. Picture books incorporating the featured letter are also listed.

Quick Review   It is important to review the letter–sound relationship learned the day before, and to review earlier concepts periodically. The quick reviews that open each lesson provide some ideas. Since students learn best when a variety of learning modalities are employed, you should vary review activities between auditory, visual, and written tasks.

Phonemic Awareness   Phonemic awareness is a key predictor of later reading success. The oral activities in this section help students recognize, think about, and work with the regular sounds of the consonants. Each lesson describes one activity, though teachers may choose to reinforce the skills with any combination of oral activities. Throughout this guide, students build phonemic awareness through isolating, identifying, categorizing, and segmenting phonemes. Books A, B, and C focus on initial consonant sounds, and Book C also incorporates work with final consonant sounds.

Phonics   This section introduces students to the letter–sound relationships of the consonants. The activities reinforce the alphabetic principle and build a foundation for later decoding of words. Each new letter–sound relationship is introduced through familiar objects or pictures. Students practice chants to help them remember the key word for each consonant, and they think about other words that start with the same sound and letter. The *Explode The Code* Wall Chart and Picture–Letter Cards feature the key words from each lesson and provide visual reinforcement for instruction.

Vocabulary

Introduce New Vocabulary   Learning new words is essential to the development of reading comprehension. This section lists the new vocabulary words from the lesson and directs teachers to clarify understanding of these words, as necessary.

Direction Words   In Books A, B, and C, students are asked to: color objects; trace, copy, and write letters; follow a path with a pencil; circle letters; draw objects; work with colors; identify numbers 1, 2, and 3; and understand meanings of *same/different, below,* and *left/right*. Confirm students' understanding of these words through discussion and example. You may also play a game like Simon Says to reinforce understanding: "Simon Says put your thumbs *up*, thumbs *down, left* hand on head, *right* leg in front, put hand in *same* place, put leg in *different* place, put arm *over* head, put hands *under* the table," etc.

Completing Student Pages This section directs the class to the corresponding *Explode The Code* student books. Teachers read the student book directions with the class and check for understanding of the task. Each student book lesson follows a predictable format; as students learn the format, they should be able to complete the pages more independently.

Pacing Suggestions The number of pages a given class can do at one sitting depends on the individual class. Most students of this age can work purposefully with concentration for about twenty minutes. Within this time frame, a class may complete three or four pages at a time, but do not hesitate to slow it down to only two or three pages per day if necessary. Establish a pace that is comfortable for your classroom.

Fluency Students who are not yet reading connected text benefit from teacher modeling of fluent reading. It is suggested that teachers regularly read aloud to their students, modeling left to right tracking and appropriate expression.

Comprehension Reading aloud from a wonderful picture book instills a love of reading and motivates students to listen for meaning. Students who are not yet reading connected text benefit from teacher modeling of comprehension strategies. Read-aloud comprehension strategies suggested in this guide include retelling, predicting, and visualizing. Students are also given opportunities to extend word knowledge and apply language skills by discussing new vocabulary words and using new words in sentences.

Writing (Letter Formation) Writing goes hand-in-hand with phonics instruction. Students need multiple opportunities to practice correct formation of each new letter. This section provides a number of fun and multisensory suggestions for reinforcing letter formation.

Reinforcement Activities This section provides suggestions for interactive reinforcement of the skills in each lesson. The activities and games offer a variety of visual, auditory, and kinesthetic options. Several activities incorporate cumulative review of letters and sounds from earlier lessons.

Explode The Code Coordinating Materials

Explode The Code **Placement Test** The tests in this quick assessment help teachers determine student placement within the *Explode The Code* series.

Picture–Letter Cards The *Ready, Set, Go* Picture–Letter Cards feature initial consonants taught in Books A, B, and C. The set consists of twenty-one sheets, each with a picture card, a letter card, and a picture card with the letter superimposed.

Wall Chart and Activity Book The *Explode The Code* Wall Chart is a colorful felt wall chart with letter pockets containing tangible felt objects that reinforce the key words for the twenty-six letters of the alphabet and their sounds. The Activity Book for the Wall Chart provides ideas for several activities and games to further aid in learning the names and sounds of the letters taught in Books A, B, C, and 1.

Explode The Code **Code Cards** This set of fifty-four index cards reinforces the sound–symbol relationships taught in *Explode The Code* Books 1–3. Code Cards can be used for instruction and review.

Explode The Code for English Language Learners This resource supplements instruction of *Explode The Code* Books 1–3 by providing specific direction for teachers of English language learners. Reproducible student pages are included.

Explode The Code **Extra Practice Books** *Explode The Code* Books 1½–6½ provide further practice in the skills taught in Books 1–6.

Beyond The Code The *Beyond The Code* books provide opportunities for advanced reading of longer stories. These books incorporate skills from the *Explode The Code* books, introduce many more sight words, and emphasize reading comprehension and critical thinking.

Get Ready for The Code
Book A

Teaching the Letter *f*
Materials: Wall Chart **fish**; Picture–Letter Cards for *f*
Picture book suggestions: *Fish is Fish* or *Frederick* by Leo Leoni

Link to Prior Knowledge

Tell the class that today they will be thinking about the sounds at the beginning of words. Ask a volunteer to say his or her name aloud. Then ask the student to say only the first sound in his or her name. Assist as necessary. Ask the class if anyone else has a name that begins with that same sound. Have students repeat names that have the same beginning sound, and isolate the beginning sound with the students.

Tell students that letters of the alphabet stand for the different sounds we hear in names and all other words. Ask the class if they can name the letter that stands for the beginning sound in the names discussed above. Then ask volunteers to say their names, the beginning sound in their names, and the letter that stands for the beginning sound in their names. Help students, as necessary.

Tell students that they are going to be learning about some other sounds and the letters of the alphabet that stand for those sounds.

Phonemic Awareness

Display the Wall Chart **fish** and ask students to name it. Have the class repeat the word *fish* several times. Then ask the class to say only the first sound in *fish* [/f/]. Have them repeat the *f* sound.

Ask the class what sound they hear at the beginning of *fox*. Is this the same sound as at the beginning of *fish*? Then ask the class to indicate with thumbs up or thumbs down if the following words begin with /f/: *feather, farm, mud, fast, shoe, finger, goat, feet, pick, rush, first.*

Phonics

Introduce the Skill   Say the word *fish*, emphasizing the initial consonant sound. Ask students if they can name the letter that stands for the sound /f/ that they hear at the beginning of *fish, feet,* and *four.*

Write the letter *f* on the board or display the *f* picture–letter card. Tell the class that this is the letter *f,* and it stands for the sound at the beginning of *fish.* Hold up the **fish** from the Wall Chart or fish picture card. Say the letter name, the sound, and key word: "*f* says /f/ as in *fish.*" Have the class repeat the phrase.

Ask students to name other words that begin like *fish,* then ask what letter the words begin with. Clarify any incorrect responses.

Vocabulary

Introduce New Vocabulary Words from this lesson include **fish, fan, football, fork, foot, fence, finger,** and **fishing.** Clarify meaning of any of these words, as necessary, during the lesson.

Review Direction Words In this and subsequent lessons, students are asked to: color objects; trace, copy, and write letters; follow a path with a pencil; circle letters; draw objects; work with colors; identify numbers 1, 2, and 3; and understand meanings of *same/ different, below,* and *left/right.* Review the directions with the class before beginning each exercise.

Completing Student Pages 1–12

Page 1. Read the directions aloud. As necessary, assist students by asking them if all figures are pointing in the same direction.

Page 2. Model formation of the letter *f* for the class. Have students write the letter in the air as you write it on the board. Have students look at the letter *f* in the middle of the page. Then have them find the number 1 and place their index fingers on it. Ask students to start tracing the letter, beginning at number 1 and following the stroke of the first line. To continue, have them find the number 2 and follow that line. They should say the letter name and its sound as they trace it. Point out the capital letter *F* in the bottom corner of the page and tell students that capital letters are used to begin names and sentences. Reinforce letter formation with the writing suggestions provided for this lesson or by having students practice writing the letter on lined paper.

Page 3. Read the directions aloud, and remind students to work carefully. Make sure they move from left to right. Ask them to say both the word and the first sound in the word when they get to the picture. Students who have trouble staying within the lines may need more exercises to strengthen small-muscle coordination.

Page 4. Read the directions aloud. For each row, make sure students are tracking from left to right. Point out that the bottom line shows capital letters.

Page 5. Read the directions aloud, pausing for students to respond to each part. As they color the sections, have them say the letter name, the sound of the letter, and the name of the pictured word. Remind students that they are looking for both lowercase and capital letters.

Page 6. Have the class point to each picture on page 7 as you name it: **fork, fence, football, fishing, finger, fan, fish, foot.** Pause between each word, allowing students time to respond. Then read the questions below and have them follow the directions for the pictures on page 7.

1. I am thinking of something that is often made of wood. It keeps animals in a yard. What is it? [fence] Put your finger on the **fence.** What sound does **fence** begin with? Color the **fence.**

2. I am thinking of something that you plug in. It moves the hot air and makes you feel cool. What is it? [fan] Put your finger on the **fan.** What sound does **fan** begin with? Draw a circle around the **fan.**

3. Now find a picture of something that we use when we eat. What is it? [fork] Put your finger on the **fork.** What sound do you hear at the beginning of **fork**? Draw an X on the **fork.**

4. I am thinking of something that lives in water and swims with its fins. What is it? [fish] Put your finger on the **fish.** Say the sound at the beginning of **fish.** Color the **fish** many colors.

5. I am thinking of a part of the body that is attached to your leg. You each have a left one and a right one. What body part is it? [foot] Put your finger on the **foot.** What sound does **foot** begin with? Draw a shoe on the **foot.**

6. Now I am thinking of something I like to do. To do it, I need a rod, a hook, and some bait. It is fun to go _____. [fishing] Put your finger on the girl **fishing.** Have you ever gone **fishing**? What sound do you hear at the beginning of **fishing**? Draw a **fish** on the girl's hook.

7. I am thinking of something you can kick or throw. You can run with it and score a touchdown. What is it? [football] Put your finger on the **football.** What sound does **football** begin with? Color the stripes on the **football.**

8. The last picture shows a part of the hand. You can wiggle it. What is it called? [finger] Put your finger on the picture of the **finger.** What sound does **finger** begin with? Draw a box around the **finger.**

Page 7. Read the directions on page 6 aloud while students listen and work.

Page 8. Together, slowly identify all the pictures on the page. (Note: For the last picture in line four, students need to say *fishing*, not *girl*.) Read the directions aloud. Students may also mark the correct picture with an X.

Page 9. Read the directions aloud, pausing for students to complete each part. Give praise for slow, careful work.

Page 10–12. Read the directions aloud. If the directions have multiple steps, pause for students to complete each task. Identify pictures, as necessary.

Building Fluency

Modeling Fluent Reading Select a read-aloud book or a poem that features words beginning with the letter *f*. Read the book or poem several times throughout the week, modeling left to right reading and appropriate expression. After you read the book, you may ask students to recall words from the story that begin with the letter *f*.

Building Comprehension

Extending Word Knowledge Give students opportunities to talk about new words in different contexts. For example, have students talk to a partner about different situations where people would use a **fan**. Encourage examples from their own experiences.

Understanding Text After a read-aloud, reinforce understanding of the story by asking students to describe what happened in the story. Clarify order of events, as necessary. Ask students who or what the story was about and where the story happened. If the story is informational, ask students what facts they remember.

Writing

To reinforce letter formation, have students practice writing the letter *f* in the following fun way. Lightly cover the bottom of a tray or other flat surface with sand, salt, or sugar. Have students write individual letters in the tray with their fingers, making the letters as large as possible.

Reinforcement Activities

1. Have students search the classroom for objects or pictures of objects that begin with /f/. Possible answers: *folder, friends, floor, flag, finger, feet.*

2. On the board write some simple words that include the letter *f*. Ask volunteers to identify and circle the letter *f* in each word.

Teaching the Letter *b*

Materials: Wall Chart **bell**, **fish**; Picture–Letter Cards for *b*
Picture book suggestions: *Buster* by Denise Fleming; *The Baby Beebee Bird*
by Diane Redfield Massie, Steven Kellogg (illus.)

Quick Review

Display the Wall Chart **fish**. Have students name it and say the first sound [/f/]. Ask them what letter makes this sound. Then toss the **fish** to a student as you say /f/. Have the student who catches it say: "*f* says /f/ as in *fish*." Throw it a few more times to different students and have them repeat the phrase.

Phonemic Awareness

Display the Wall Chart **bell** and ask students to name it. Have the class repeat the word *bell* several times. Then ask the class to say only the first sound in *bell* [/b/]. Have students repeat the /b/ sound.

Ask the class what sound they hear at the beginning of *baby*. Is this the same sound as at the beginning of *bell*? Then ask the class to indicate with thumbs up or thumbs down if the following words begin with /b/: *bull, bank, song, bark, fish, four, band, jump, bud*.

Phonics

Introduce the Skill Say the word *bell*, emphasizing the initial consonant sound. Ask students if they can name the letter that stands for the sound /b/ that they hear at the beginning of *bell, band,* and *bag*.

Write the letter *b* on the board or show the *b* picture–letter card. Tell the class that this is the letter *b*, and it stands for the sound at the beginning of *bell*. Hold up the Wall Chart **bell** or bell picture card. Say the letter name, the sound, and key word: "*b* says /b/ as in *bell*." Have the class repeat the phrase.

Ask students to name other words that begin like *bell*, then ask what letter the words begin with. Clarify any incorrect responses.

Vocabulary

Introduce New Vocabulary Words from this lesson include **bus, belt, bike, boots, bird, balloon, basket,** and **box**. Clarify the meaning of these words, as necessary, during the lesson.

Completing Student Pages 13–24

Page 13. Read the directions aloud. Assist students, as necessary, by asking them questions about the pictures.

Page 14. Model formation of the letter *b* for the class. Have students write the letter in the air as you write it on the board. Have students look at the letter *b* in the middle of the page. Then have them find the number 1 and place their index fingers on it. Ask students to start tracing the letter, beginning at number 1 and following the stroke of the first line. To continue, have them find the number 2 and follow that line. They should say the letter name and its sound as they trace it. Point out the capital letter *B* in the bottom corner of the page and tell students that capital letters are used to begin names and sentences. Reinforce letter formation with the writing suggestions provided for this lesson or by having students practice writing the letter on lined paper.

Page 15. Read the directions aloud, and remind students to work carefully. Make sure they move from left to right. Ask them to say both the word and the first sound in the word when they get to the picture.

Page 16. Read the directions aloud. For each row, make sure students are tracking from left to right. Point out that the bottom line shows capital letters.

Page 17. Read the directions aloud, pausing for students to respond to each part. As they color the sections, have them say the letter name, the sound of the letter, and the name of the pictured word. Remind students that they are looking for both lowercase and capital letters.

Page 18. Have the class point to each picture on page 19 as you name it: **belt, bicycle, bird, box, basket, balloon, boots, bus.** Pause between each word, allowing students time to respond. Then read the questions below and have them follow the directions for the pictures on page 19.

1. I am thinking of something you buckle around your waist to hold your pants up. What is it? [belt] Put your finger on the **belt**. What sound do you hear at the beginning of **belt**? Draw an X on the **belt**.

2. I am thinking of something you wear on your feet to keep them warm and dry. What are they called? [boots] Put your finger on the **boots**. What sound do you hear at the beginning of **boots**? Color the **boots**.

3. I am thinking of something that is filled with air. It will burst if you prick it. What is it? [balloon] Put your finger on the **balloon**. What sound does **balloon** begin with? Color the **balloon** your favorite color.

4. I am thinking of something that has a handle, which makes it easy to carry many things. (But please do not try to carry water in it.) What is it called? [basket] Put your finger on the **basket**. What sound do you hear? Draw a circle around the **basket**.

5. I am thinking of something you can ride, but you must push the pedals to make it go. What is it? [bike/bicycle] Put your finger on the **bicycle**. What sound do you hear at the beginning? Draw a box around the **bicycle**.

6. Now I am thinking of something bigger than a car that you can ride in. Lots of students go to school on a school _____ [bus]. Put your finger on the **bus**. Say the word again. What sound does **bus** begin with? Color the **bus** its usual color.

7. I am thinking of something you can put things in. It sometimes has a lid so nothing falls out. It is made of cardboard. What is it called? [box] Put your finger on the **box**. What sound do you hear at the beginning of **box**? Color the lid of the **box**.

8. The last picture is of something with wings. It builds a nest to lay its eggs in. What is it? [bird] Put your finger on the **bird**. You may color the **bird** any color you like, but do it carefully.

Page 19. Read the directions aloud on page 18 while students listen and work.

Page 20. Read the directions aloud and assist students, as necessary.

Page 21. Read the directions aloud, pausing for students to complete each part. Give praise for slow, careful work.

Page 22–24. Read the directions aloud, pausing for students to complete each task. Identify pictures, as necessary.

Building Fluency

Modeling Fluent Reading Select a read-aloud book or a poem that features words beginning with the letter *b*. Read the book or poem several times throughout the week, modeling left to right reading and appropriate expression. After you read the book, you may ask students to recall words from the story that begin with the letter *b*.

Building Comprehension

Using Language Review any new words from the lesson or read-aloud. Ask volunteers to use one of the new words in a sentence.

Prediction As you read aloud to the class, pause at various points throughout the story to ask students what they think will happen next. Confirm correct predictions as you read the rest of the story.

Writing

To reinforce letter formation, have students practice writing the letter *b* in the following fun way. Cut a piece of sandpaper in half and write a letter on each piece. Have students trace the letter with their index fingers.

Reinforcement Activities

1. Divide the class into two teams. Ask each team to tell you whether the words you say begin with /f/ or /b/. Use simple words such as: *bug, fly, flea, band, bean, floor,* and *box.*

2. On the board write some simple words that include the letters *b* or *f*. Ask a volunteer to identify and circle those letters in each word.

Teaching the Letter *m*

Materials: Wall Chart fish, bell, mitten and three other objects; Picture–Letter Cards for **m**
Picture book suggestions: *Missing Molly* by Lisa Jahn-Clough; *If You Give a Moose a Muffin* by Laura Numeroff; *The Mitten* by Jan Brett

Quick Review

Have students tell you which letter says /b/. Then ask them to name the key word for the letter *b* [*bell*]. Hold up the Wall Chart **bell**. Toss the **bell** to a student as you say /b/. Have the student who catches it say: "*b* says /b/ as in *bell*." Throw it a few more times along with the *fish*, and have different students respond each time.

Phonemic Awareness

Display the Wall Chart **mitten** and ask students to name it. Have the class repeat the word *mitten* several times. Then ask the class to say only the first sound in *mitten* [/m/]. Have them repeat the /m/ sound.

   Ask the class what sound they hear at the beginning of *mother*. Is this the same sound as at the beginning of *mitten*? Then ask the class to indicate with thumbs up or thumbs down if the following words begin with /m/: *mint, man, mice, tree, mask, goat, mouth, kitten, marker, map, magazine.*

Phonics

Introduce the Skill Say the word *mitten*, emphasizing the initial consonant sound. Ask students if they can name the letter that stands for the sound /m/ that they hear at the beginning of *mitten, Monday,* and *milk.*

   Write the letter *m* on the board or show the m picture–letter card. Tell the class that this is the letter *m*, and it stands for the sound at the beginning of *mitten*. Hold up the Wall Chart **mitten** or mitten picture card. Say the letter name, the sound, and key word: "*m* says /m/ as in *mitten*." Have the class repeat the phrase.

   Ask students to name other words that begin like *mitten*, then ask what letter the words begin with. Clarify any incorrect responses.

Vocabulary

Introduce New Vocabulary Words from this lesson include **mountain, mouse, moon, monkey, monster, money,** and **mittens**. Clarify the meaning of these words, as necessary, during the lesson.

Completing Student Pages 25-38

Page 25. Read the directions aloud and assist students, as necessary.

Page 26. Model formation of the letter *m* for the class. Have students write the letter in the air as you write it on the board. Have students look at the letter *m* in the middle of the page. Then have them find the number 1 and place their index fingers on it. Ask students to start tracing the letter, beginning at number 1 and following the stroke of the first line. To continue, have them find the number 2 and follow that line. Then have them find the number 3 and follow that line. They should say the letter and its sound as they trace it. Point out the capital letter *M* in the bottom corner of the page and tell students that capital letters are used to begin names and sentences. Reinforce letter formation with the writing suggestions provided for this lesson or by having students practice writing the letter on lined paper.

Page 27. Read the directions aloud. Make sure students move from left to right. Ask them to say the word and the first sound in the word when they get to the picture.

Page 28. Read the directions aloud. For each row, make sure students are tracking from left to right. Point out that the bottom line shows capital letters.

Page 29. Read the directions aloud, pausing for students to respond to each part. As they color the sections, have them say the letter name, the sound of the letter, and the name of the pictured word. Remind students that they are looking for both lowercase and capital letters.

Page 30. Have the class point to each picture on page 31 as you name it: **mountain, moon, monster, mittens, money, monkey, mouse**. Pause between each word, allowing students time to respond. Then read the questions below and have them follow the directions for the pictures on page 31.

1. I am thinking of something you can use to buy things. You keep it in your purse or wallet or sometimes in a bank. What is it? [money] Put your finger on the **money**. What sound does **money** begin with? Draw a square around the **money**.

2. I am thinking of a clever animal that uses its fingers and toes to swing in trees. It also likes to eat bananas. What animal am I thinking of? [monkey] Put your finger on the **monkey**. What sound do you hear at the beginning of **monkey**? Color the **monkey**.

3. Now find a picture of something that glows brightly in the sky at night. Astronauts walked on it. What is it? [moon] Put your finger on the **moon**. What sound do you hear at the beginning of **moon**? Color the **moon** yellow.

4. I am thinking of something you put on your hands to keep them warm in winter. You should wear these when you make snowballs. What are they called? [mittens] Put your finger on the **mittens**. Say the sound at the beginning of **mittens**. Draw a circle around one **mitten**.

5. The creature in this picture looks terrible and makes you feel afraid. We call this a /m/_____ [monster]. What sound does **monster** begin with? Put your finger on the **monster**. Draw a box around the **monster**.

6. This picture shows something very, very high. When we climb to the top of one of these, we can see a long way. What do we call this tall thing? [mountain] Put your finger on the **mountain**. What does **mountain** begin with? Color the **mountain** green.

7. Find the picture we have not talked about. This is a picture of a small animal that sometimes gets into cupboards and chews holes in boxes of food. It also likes to eat cheese. It squeaks and runs fast when it sees you. Its name begins with /m/. What is its name? [mouse] Put your finger on the **mouse**. Color the **mouse** any way you'd like.

Page 31. Read the directions aloud on page 30 while students listen and work.

Page 32. Read the directions aloud and assist students, as necessary.

Page 33. Read the directions aloud, pausing for students to complete each part. Give praise for slow, careful work.

Page 34. Read the directions aloud. Identify pictures, as necessary.

Page 35–38. Read the directions aloud, pausing for students to complete each task. Identify pictures, as necessary.

Building Fluency

Modeling Fluent Reading Select a read-aloud book or a poem that features words beginning with the letter *m*. Read the book or poem several times throughout the week, modeling left to right reading and appropriate expression. After you read the book, you may ask students to recall words from the story that begin with the letter *m*.

Building Comprehension

Extending Word Knowledge Give students opportunities to talk about new words in different contexts. For example, have students talk to a partner about **mittens**, and other clothing they might wear in cold weather. For the word **mountain**, have students explain how a hill and mountain are different.

Understanding Text After a read-aloud, reinforce understanding of the story by asking students to describe what happened in the story. Clarify order of events, as necessary. Ask students who or what the story was about and where the story happened. If the story is informational, ask students what facts they remember.

Writing

To reinforce letter formation, have students practice writing the letter *m* in the following fun way. Direct students to use their index fingers to write the letter *m* on the floor, then on the desk, rug, wall, table, and chair—the more texture to the surface the better!

Reinforcement Activities

1. Divide the class into two teams. Ask each team to tell you whether the word you say begins with /f/, /m/, or /b/. (For more of a challenge, you can ask them to tell whether the word begins with the letter *f, m,* or *b*.) Use simple words such as: *bug, fly, mad, mean, flea, band, bean, moth, floor, box.*

2. Place the Wall Chart **fish, mitten,** and **bell,** and three other objects in a row. Tell the class to look carefully at the row. Have them cover their eyes while you remove one object. Then ask students which object is missing. Repeat two or three times. When the **fish, mitten,** and **bell** are removed and identified as missing, ask the class what sound and letter each word begins with.

Teaching the Letter *k*

Materials: Wall Chart **mitten, bell, fish,** and **kite**; Picture–Letter Cards for *k*
Picture book suggestion: *What Do You Do with a Kangaroo?* by Mercer Mayer

Quick Review

Display the letter *m*. Have students name it, and tell what sound it makes [/m/]. Then ask them to name the key word that starts with /m/ [*mitten*]. Hold up the Wall Chart **mitten** and have students say: "*m* says /m/ as in *mitten*." Continue with the letters *b* and *f*. Then call on individual students to repeat the exercise.

Phonemic Awareness

Display the Wall Chart **kite** and ask students to name it. Have the whole class repeat the word *kite* several times. Then ask the class to say only the first sound in *kite* [/k/]. Have them repeat the /k/ sound.

    Ask the class what sound they hear at the beginning of *kitten*. Is this the same sound as at the beginning of *kite*? Then ask the class to indicate with thumbs up or thumbs down if the following words begin with /k/: *tap, kiss, keep, game, bath, king, time, sand, key, fall, kind.*

Phonics

Introduce the Skill Say the word *kite*, emphasizing the initial consonant sound. Ask students if they can name the letter that stands for the sound /k/ that they hear at the beginning of *kite, kitten, keep, kind, key,* and *kiss.*

Write the letter *k* on the board or display the *k* picture–letter card. Tell the class that this is the letter *k,* and it stands for the sound at the beginning of *kite.* Hold up the Wall Chart **kite** or kite picture card. Say the letter name, the sound, and key word: "*k* says /k/ as in *kite.*" Have the class repeat the phrase.

Ask students to name other words that begin like *kite,* and then ask what letter the words begin with. Clarify any incorrect responses.

Vocabulary

Introduce New Vocabulary Words from this lesson include **kitten, king, kiss, kite, key, kick,** and **kangaroo.** Clarify the meaning of these words, as necessary, during the lesson.

Completing Student Pages 39–52

Page 39. Read the directions aloud and assist students, as necessary.

Page 40. Model formation of the letter *k* for the class. Have students write the letter in the air as you write it on the board. Have students look at the letter *k* in the middle of the page. Then have them find the number 1 and place their index fingers on it. Ask students to start tracing the letter, beginning at number 1 and following the stroke of the first line. To continue, have them find the number 2 and follow that line. They should say the letter and its sound as they trace it. Point out the capital letter *K* in the bottom corner of the page and tell students that capital letters are used to begin names and sentences. Reinforce letter formation with the writing suggestions provided for this lesson or by having students practice writing the letter on lined paper.

Page 41. Read the directions aloud. Make sure students move from left to right. Ask them to say both the word and the first sound in the word when they get to the picture.

Page 42. Read the directions aloud. Make sure students are tracking from left to right. Point out that the bottom line shows capital letters.

Page 43. Read the directions aloud and assist students, as necessary.

Page 44. Have the class point to each picture on page 45 as you name it: **king, kiss, kangaroo, kick, kite, key, kitten.** Pause between each word, allowing students time to respond. Then read the questions below and have them follow the directions for the pictures on page 45.

1. I am thinking of something you use to unlock a door. It is made of metal and fits in a small hole. What is it? [key] Put your finger on the **key.** What sound do you hear at the beginning of **key?** Color the **key.**

2. I am thinking of something that is fun to do with a ball. You use your foot to do this. What is the word? [kick] Put your finger on the picture for **kick.** What sound do you hear at the beginning of **kick?** Draw a circle around the ball.

3. I am thinking of something that can go up high in the sky if there is a lot of wind. But be sure you hold on to the string! What is it? [kite] Put your finger on the **kite.** Draw a longer tail on the **kite.**

4. I am thinking of an animal that lives in Australia. The mother carries her baby in her pouch. When she takes big hops, the baby stays safe inside the pouch. What animal am I thinking of? [kangaroo] Put your finger on the **kangaroo.** What sound does **kangaroo** begin with? Color just the tail of the **kangaroo.**

5. I am thinking of a man who wears a crown and sits on a throne. He is a _____ [king]. Put your finger on the **king** and draw a circle around him.

6. Now I am thinking of something small and soft and fluffy. It makes a tiny mewing noise when it is hungry. What is the name for a baby cat? [kitten] Put your finger on the **kitten.** What sound does **kitten** begin with? Draw a collar on the **kitten.**

7. The picture we have not talked about yet shows two people who like each other. They are puckering up their lips to give each other a big /k/_____ [kiss]. Put your finger on the picture of the **kiss.** What sound does **kiss** begin with? Color this picture any way you wish.

Page 45. Read the directions aloud on page 44 while students listen and work.

Page 46. Read the directions aloud and assist students, as necessary.

Page 47. Read the directions aloud, pausing for students to complete each part. Give praise for slow, careful work.

Page 48. Together, identify the pictures. Read the directions aloud. Students may also mark the correct picture with an X.

Page 49–52. Read the directions aloud. If the directions have multiple steps, pause for students to complete each task. Identify pictures, as necessary.

Building Fluency

Modeling Fluent Reading Select a read-aloud book or a poem that features words beginning with the letter *k*. Read the book or poem several times throughout the week, modeling left to right reading and appropriate expression.

Building Comprehension

Using Language Review any new words from the lesson or read-aloud. Ask volunteers to use one of the new words in a sentence.

Visualization Read a new picture book to the class without showing the pictures. Explain that they should make a picture in their minds about what is happening in the story as they listen. Ask students to describe how they imagine the characters and places to look. Read the story a second time, showing the pictures. As you read, ask students to describe how the pictures were similar to or different from the pictures they had visualized.

Writing

To reinforce letter formation, have students practice writing the letter *k* in the following fun way. Put a small amount of shaving cream on a tray or other flat surface, and have students use their index fingers to write letters.

Reinforcement Activities

1. Make and distribute one *f, b, m,* or *k* letter card to each student. Write a letter on the board. Ask all students with that letter to come to the front of the class. Have one volunteer from that group name the letter, and another name the sound. Ask other students to name words that begin with that sound.

2. For each group of words below, have students identify what first sound is the same and what letter makes that sound: *kitten kite king; fish fan finger; ball bell bird; mitten monkey mountain; key kick kangaroo; fun find fell; mouse mend middle.*

Teaching the Letter *t*

Materials: Wall Chart turkey, kite, fish, mitten, bell; Picture–Letter Cards for *t*
Picture book suggestion: *Tikki Tikki Tembo* by Arlene Mosel, Blair Lent (illus.)

Quick Review

Display the Wall Chart **kite**. Have students name it and say the first sound [/k/]. Ask them what letter makes this sound. Then toss the **kite** to a student as you say /k/. Have the student who catches it say: "*k* says /k/ as in *kite*." Throw it a few more times along with the **fish, bell,** and **mitten,** and have different students respond each time.

Phonemic Awareness

Display the Wall Chart **turkey** and ask students to name it. Have the class repeat the word *turkey* several times. Then ask the class to say only the first sound in *turkey* [/t/]. Have them repeat the /t/ sound.

Ask the class what sound they hear at the beginning of *tickle*. Is this the same sound as at the beginning of *turkey*? Then ask the class to indicate with thumbs up or thumbs down if the following words begin with /t/: *time, tongue, desk, gem, task, toad, tool, dime, table, teacher, tape, work, teeth, toes, milk*.

Phonics

Introduce the Skill Say the word *turkey*, emphasizing the initial consonant sound. Ask students if they can name the letter that stands for the sound /t/ that they hear at the beginning of *turkey, table, teacher,* and *ten*.

Write the letter *t* on the board or display the *t* picture–letter card. Tell the class that this is the letter *t*, and it stands for the sound at the beginning of *turkey*. Hold up the Wall Chart **turkey** or turkey picture card. Say the letter name, the sound, and key word: "*t* says /t/ as in *turkey*." Have the class repeat the phrase.

Ask students to name other words that begin like *turkey*, then ask what letter the words begin with. Clarify any incorrect responses.

Vocabulary

Introduce New Vocabulary Words from this lesson include **turtle, television, tail, toe, toaster, tiger, toothbrush,** and **tent**. Clarify the meaning of these words, as necessary, during the lesson.

Completing Student Pages 53–64

Page 53. Read the directions aloud and assist students, as necessary.

Page 54. Model formation of the letter *t* for the class. Have students write the letter in the air as you write it on the board. Have students look at the letter *t* in the middle of the page. Then have them find the number 1 and place their index fingers on it. Ask students to start tracing the letter, beginning at number 1 and following the stroke of the first line. To continue, have them find the number 2 and follow that line. They should say the letter and its sound as they trace it. Point out the capital letter *T* in the bottom corner of the page and tell students that capital letters are used to begin names and sentences. Reinforce letter formation with the writing suggestions provided for this lesson or by having students practice writing the letter on lined paper.

Page 55. Read the directions aloud. Make sure students move from left to right. Ask them to say both the word and the first sound in the word when they get to the picture.

Page 56. Read the directions aloud. Make sure students are tracking from left to right. Point out that the bottom line shows capital letters.

Page 57. Read the directions aloud and assist students, as necessary.

Page 58. Have the class point to each picture on page 59 as you name it: **television, tail, toaster, tent, toothbrush, tiger, toe, turtle.** Pause between each word, allowing students time to respond. Then read the questions below and have them follow the directions for the pictures on page 59.

1. I am thinking of something you use to clean your teeth. It has a handle with a brush at the end. What is it? [toothbrush] Put your finger on the **toothbrush.** What sound do you hear at the beginning of **toothbrush**? Draw toothpaste on the **toothbrush.**

2. I am thinking of a part of the body. A person's foot has five of these. Say the word [toe]. Put your finger on the **toe.** What sound do you hear at the beginning of **toe**? Color in just the toenail.

3. I am thinking of an animal with stripes. It lives in the jungle. What is it? [tiger] Put your finger on the **tiger.** Say the sound you hear at the beginning of **tiger.** Draw a circle around the **tiger.**

4. Many animals have these. Horses and cows swish theirs to keep away flies. Dogs wag theirs when they are happy. What am I thinking of? [tail] Put your finger on the **tail.** What sound does **tail** begin with? Draw an X on the **tail.**

5. I am thinking of an animal that moves very slowly. It is protected by a hard shell. What animal am I thinking of? [turtle] Put your finger on the **turtle.** What sound does **turtle** begin with? Color the **turtle.**

6. Now I am thinking of something you sleep in when you go camping. It has two flaps for doors and is often held up by poles and rope. What is this thing called? [tent] Put your finger on the **tent.** What sound does **tent** begin with? Draw another rope to make the **tent** stronger.

7. I am thinking of something you use in the kitchen. It makes a snack by heating bread until it is crisp. What is it called? [toaster] Put your finger on the **toaster.** What sound does **toaster** begin with? Draw a piece of toast coming out of the **toaster.**

8. The last picture is of something you can turn on and off. You can watch your favorite programs on it. What is its name? [television] Put your finger on the **television.** What sound does **television** begin with? Draw on the **television** screen something you might see on TV.

Page 59. Read the directions aloud on page 58 while students listen and work.

Page 60. Read the directions aloud and assist students, as necessary.

Page 61. Read the directions aloud, pausing for students to complete each part. Give praise for slow, careful work.

Pages 62–64. Read the directions aloud. If the directions have multiple steps, pause for students to complete each task. Identify pictures, as necessary.

Building Fluency

Modeling Fluent Reading Select a read-aloud book or a poem that features words beginning with the letter *t*. Read the book or poem several times throughout the week, modeling left to right reading and appropriate expression.

Building Comprehension

Extending Word Knowledge Give students opportunities to talk about new words in different contexts. For example, have students talk to a partner about the different kinds of **tails** animals have. How is a horse's tail different from a cat's tail? from a pig's tail?

Understanding Text After a read-aloud, reinforce understanding of the story by asking students to describe what happened in the story. Clarify order of events, as necessary. Ask students who or what the story was about and where the story happened. If the story is informational, ask students what facts they remember.

Writing

To reinforce letter formation, have students practice writing the letter *t* in the following fun way. Bring in a straw mat, a small rag rug, or a piece of screening, and have students draw the letter *t* on it with their fingers.

Reinforcement Activities

1. Divide the class into two teams. Ask them to tell you whether the word you say begins with /k/ or /t/. (You can also ask them to tell you if the word begins with the letter *t* or the letter *k*.) Use simple words such as: *toy, keep, kitten, tool, kayak, target, top,* and *key*.

2. Working with letters learned thus far, provide each student with a card set of lowercase letters and a card set of capital letters. Have students match each lowercase letter with its corresponding capital letter.

Teaching the Letter *r*

Materials: Wall Chart **kite, rocket, fish, mitten, turkey, bell,** and three other objects;
Picture–Letter Cards for *r, t, k, b, f, m*
Picture book suggestion: *My Friend Rabbit* by Eric Rohman

Quick Review

Ask students to listen and tell you what letter says /t/ [t]. Then ask them to name the key word for the letter *t* [*turkey*]. Hold up the Wall Chart **turkey.** Then toss the **turkey** to a student as you say /t/. Have the student who catches it say: "*t* says /t/ as in *turkey*." Throw it a few more times along with the **bell, kite, fish,** and **mitten,** and have different students respond each time.

Phonemic Awareness

Display the Wall Chart **rocket** and ask students to name it. Have the class repeat the word *rocket* several times. Then ask the class to say only the first sound in *rocket* [/r/]. Have them repeat the /r/ sound.

Ask the class what sound they hear at the beginning of *ranch*. Is this the same sound as at the beginning of *rocket*? Then ask the class to indicate with thumbs up or thumbs down if the following words begin with /r/: *rest, run, rip, sip, rent, test, ripe, rug, walk, radio, girl, rule, reader.*

Phonics

Introduce the Skill Say the word *rocket*, emphasizing the initial consonant sound. Ask students if they can name the letter that stands for the sound /r/ that they hear at the beginning of *rocket, red, rule,* and *run*.

Write the letter *r* on the board or show the *r* picture–letter card. Tell the class that this is the letter *r*, and it stands for the sound at the beginning of *rocket*. Hold up the Wall Chart **rocket** or rocket picture card. Say the letter name, the sound, and key word: "*r* says /r/ as in *rocket*." Have the class repeat the phrase.

Ask students to name other words that begin like *rocket*, then ask what letter the words begin with. Clarify any incorrect responses.

Vocabulary

Introduce New Vocabulary Words from this lesson include **radio, rain, rake, ring, rope, rabbit, rocket,** and **rainbow.** Clarify meaning of these words, as necessary, during the lesson.

Completing Student Pages 65–78

Page 65. Read the directions aloud and assist students, as necessary.

Page 66. Model formation of the letter *r* for the class. Have students write the letter in the air as you write it on the board. Have students look at the letter *r* in the middle of the page. Then have them find the number 1 and place their index fingers on it. Ask students to start tracing the letter, beginning at number 1 and following the stroke of the first line. To continue, have them find the number 2 and follow that line. They should say the letter and its sound as they trace it. Point out the capital letter *R* in the bottom corner of the page and remind students that capital letters are used to begin names and sentences. Reinforce letter formation with the writing suggestions provided for this lesson or by having students practice writing the letter on lined paper.

Page 67. Read the directions aloud. Make sure students move from left to right. Ask them to say both the word and the first sound in the word when they get to the picture.

Page 68. Read the directions aloud. For each row, make sure students are tracking from left to right. Point out to students that the bottom line shows capital letters.

Page 69. Read the directions aloud, pausing for students to respond to each part. As they color the sections, have them say the letter name, the sound of the letter, and the name of the pictured word. Remind students that they are looking for both lowercase and capital letters.

Page 70. Have the class point to each picture on page 71 as you name it: **rain, rake, rope, rainbow, rocket, rabbit, ring, radio.** Pause between each word, allowing students time to respond. Then read the questions below and have them follow the directions for the pictures on page 71.

1. I am thinking of something you can listen to. You may hear music, the news, or a weather report. What am I thinking of? [radio] Put your finger on the **radio.** What sound does **radio** begin with? Draw a circle around the **radio.**

2. I am thinking of an animal with long ears and a short, fuzzy tail. This animal hops, and its babies are called bunnies. What is this animal called? [rabbit] Put your finger on the **rabbit.** What sound do you hear at the beginning of **rabbit**? Draw a carrot in front of the **rabbit.**

3. What would you use to tie up a boat? to swing from a tree? to pull something heavy? I am thinking of a _____. [rope] Put your finger on the **rope.** What sound does **rope** begin with? Make the **rope** look like a snake.

4. Sometimes the sun goes behind the clouds and suddenly you feel drops falling. What are these drops? [rain] Put your finger on the **rain.** What sound do you hear at the beginning of **rain**? Color the clouds, but not the **rain.**

5. I am thinking of something you can wear on your finger. When it has a diamond or another jewel in it, it sparkles. What is this piece of jewelry called? [ring] Put your finger on the **ring**. Say the sound you hear at the beginning of **ring**. Draw a box around the **ring**.

6. You use this to collect leaves into a pile in the fall and to clean out gardens in the springtime. What is this tool called? [rake] Put your finger on the **rake**. What sound does **rake** begin with? Have you ever used a **rake**? Color its handle.

7. Find the picture that shows something shooting into the air at high speed. Its name begins with /r/. What is it? [rocket] Put your finger on the **rocket**. Say the beginning sound of **rocket**. Then color the **rocket** red.

8. The last picture shows something we don't see very often. Sometimes when the sun comes out after it has been raining, a beautiful, colorful reflection is seen in the sky. Some people think there is a pot of gold at the end of it. What is this multicolored vision called? [rainbow] Put your finger on the **rainbow**. What sound does **rainbow** begin with? Color the **rainbow** many beautiful colors.

Page 71. Read the directions aloud on page 70 while students listen and work.

Page 72. Together, slowly identify all the pictures on the page. Read the directions aloud. Students may also mark the correct picture with an X.

Page 73. Read the directions aloud, pausing for students to complete each part. Give praise for slow, careful work.

Page 74–78. Read the directions aloud. If the directions have multiple steps, pause for students to complete each task.

Building Fluency

Modeling Fluent Reading Select a read-aloud book or a poem that features words beginning with the letter r. Read the book or poem several times throughout the week, modeling left to right reading and appropriate expression.

Building Comprehension

Using Language Review any new words from the lesson or read-aloud. Ask volunteers to use one of the new words in a sentence.

Prediction As you read aloud to the class, pause at various points throughout the story to ask students what they think will happen next. Confirm correct predictions as you read the rest of the story.

Writing

To reinforce letter formation, have students practice writing the letter *r* in the following fun ways. 1) Provide whiteboards for each student and have them write the letter as large as possible with the marker provided. Then have all students display their boards at the same time to show the accuracy of their letters. Repeat with other letters students have learned. 2) Provide students with a red crayon or marker and have them practice writing the letter *r* on a light-colored piece of paper. Point out that the word *red* begins with the letter *r*.

Reinforcement Activities

1. Play Pick a Picture. Place the *b, f, m, k, t,* and *r* picture cards along the front of the board. Then say a word, such as *tiger*, and call on a student. Have the student go to the board and point to the picture with the same beginning sound as *tiger* [turkey]. Continue with other words until all students have had a turn.

2. Place the Wall Chart **fish, mitten, kite, rocket, turkey,** and **bell** and three other Wall Chart objects in a row. Tell the class to look carefully at the row. Have students cover their eyes while you remove one object, then ask which object is missing. Repeat this procedure two or three times. When the **fish, mitten, kite, rocket, turkey,** and **bell** are removed and identified as missing, ask the class what letter and sound begins each word.

3. Ask students to tell you the first sound they hear in words beginning with *b, f, m, k, t* and *r*. For example: "The first part of **rocket** is _____" [/r/]. Possible words: *face, tour, radio, fuzz, bill, keep, both, make, milk, king, mend, row, boss, range, radio, kiss, film, tear, tall, moon.*

   For additional reinforcement, play some of the games described in the *Explode The Code* Wall Chart Activity Book. Playing short games at different times of the day helps reinforce learning and make it fun. This activity book describes thirty-five different games that can be played using the Wall Chart objects.

Get Ready for The Code
Book B

Teaching the Letter *p*

Materials: Wall Chart **pear, fish, bell, kite, mitten, turkey, rocket;**
Picture–Letter Cards for *p*
Picture book suggestions: *Lilly's Purple Plastic Purse* by Kevin Henkes; *If You Give a Pig a Pancake* by Laura Numeroff, Felicia Bond (illus.); *The Popcorn Book* by Tomie DePaola

Quick Review

Display the Wall Chart **rocket**. Have students name it, then say only the first sound [/r/]. Ask what letter makes this sound. Toss the **rocket** to a student as you say /r/. Have the student who catches it say: "*r* says /r/ as in *rocket*." Throw it a few more times along with the **bell, fish, kite, mitten,** and **turkey,** and have different students respond each time.

Phonemic Awareness

Display the Wall Chart **pear** and ask students to name it. Have the class repeat the word *pear* several times. Then ask the class to say only the first sound in pear [/p/]. Have students repeat the /p/ sound.

Ask the class what sound they hear at the beginning of *paper*. Is this the same sound as at the beginning of *pear*? Then ask the class to indicate with thumbs up or thumbs down if the following words begin with /p/: *pumpkin, last, puppy, purse, bird, paste, pig, dust, pencil, little, pen, picture, pocket.*

Phonics

Introduce the Skill Say the word *pear*, emphasizing the initial consonant sound. Ask students if they can name the letter that stands for the sound /p/ that they hear at the beginning of *pear, pig, paper,* and *pencil*.

Write the letter *p* on the board or show the *p* picture–letter card. Tell the class that this is the letter *p*, and it stands for the sound at the beginning of *pear*. Hold up the Wall Chart **pear** or pear picture card. Say the letter name, the sound, and key word: "*p* says /p/ as in *pear*." Have the class repeat the phrase.

Ask students to name other words that begin like *pear*, and then ask what letter the words begin with. Clarify any incorrect responses.

Vocabulary

Introduce New Vocabulary Words from this lesson include **pig, pencil, paint, pear, pants, pie, purse**. Clarify the meaning of these words, as necessary, during the lesson.

Review Direction Words In this and subsequent lessons, students are asked to: color objects; trace, copy, and write letters; follow a path with a pencil; circle letters; draw objects; work with colors; identify numbers 1, 2, and 3; and understand meanings of *same/ different, below,* and *left/right*. Review the directions with the class before beginning each exercise.

Completing Student Pages 1–14

Page 1. Read the directions aloud and assist students, as necessary.

Page 2. Model formation of the letter *p* for the class. Have students write the letter in the air as you write it on the board. Have students look at the letter *p* in the middle of the page. Tell them to notice that *p* hangs below the line. Then have them find the number 1 and place their index fingers on it. Ask students to start tracing the letter, beginning at number 1 and following the stroke of the first line. To continue, have them find the number 2 and follow that line. They should say the letter and its sound as they trace it. Point out the capital letter *P* in the bottom corner of the page. Tell the students that capital letters are two spaces tall and are used to begin names and sentences. Reinforce letter formation with the writing suggestions provided for this lesson or by having students practice writing the letter on lined paper.

Page 3. Read the directions aloud. Make sure students move from left to right. Ask them to say both the word and the first sound in the word when they get to the picture.

Page 4. Read the directions aloud. Make sure students are tracking from left to right. Point out that the bottom line shows capital letters.

Page 5. Read the directions aloud, pausing for students to respond to each part. As they color the sections, have them say the letter name, the sound of the letter, and the name of the pictured word. Remind students that they are looking for both lowercase and capital letters.

Page 6. Have the class point to each picture on page 7 as you name it: **pencil, paints, pants, purse, pie, pear, pig**. Pause between each word, allowing students time to respond. Then read the questions below and have them follow the directions for the pictures on page 7.

1. I am thinking of something that tastes delicious. It has a crust and is baked in the oven. When you cut it into slices everyone in the family can have a piece. I am thinking of a _____ [pie]. Put your finger on the **pie**. What sound do you hear at the beginning of **pie**? Color the **pie** red.

2. I am thinking of something you use to write your name. It sometimes has an eraser on the end. What is it? [pencil] Put your finger on the **pencil**. What sound does **pencil** begin with? Color the **pencil** blue.

3. Now I am thinking of an animal. It is sometimes pink, and loves to lie in the mud. What is it? [pig] Put your finger on the **pig**. What sound does **pig** begin with? Draw mud around the **pig's** feet.

4. This juicy and delicious fruit grows on a tree. It is either brown or greenish yellow when it is ripe. This fruit is rounded at one end and smaller at the other end. What is this fruit called? [pear] Put your finger on the **pear**. What sound does **pear** begin with? Put a big X on the **pear**.

5. Find something on this page that you wear to cover your legs. Sometimes we call them trousers, but usually we call them ____ [pants]. Put your finger on the **pants**. What sound does **pants** begin with? Color the pockets on the **pants**.

6. When you want to create a beautiful, colorful picture, you might use these. You use a brush and water with them. What are they called? [paints] Put your finger on the **paints**. What sound do you hear at the beginning of **paints**? Draw two circles around the **paints**.

7. There is one picture left. Look at it. This is something people can keep their money in. What is it? [purse] Put your finger on the **purse**. Draw a wider strap on the **purse** so it won't fall off your shoulder.

Page 7. Read the directions aloud on page 6 while students listen and work.

Page 8. Read the directions aloud and assist students, as necessary.

Page 9. Read the directions aloud, pausing for students to complete each part. Give praise for slow, careful work.

Page 10–14. Read the directions aloud on page 6 and assist students, as necessary. If the directions have multiple steps, pause for students to complete each task.

Building Fluency

Modeling Fluent Reading   Select a read-aloud book or a poem that features words beginning with the letter *p*. Read the book or poem several times throughout the week, modeling left to right reading and appropriate expression. After you read the book, you may ask students to recall words from the story that begin with the letter *p*.

Building Comprehension

Extending Word Knowledge Give students opportunities to talk about new words in different contexts. For example, for the word **pear** have students work with a partner to name other kinds of fruits. Are apples like pears? Why or why not?

Understanding Text After a read-aloud, reinforce understanding of the story by asking students to describe what happened in the story. Clarify order of events, as necessary. Ask students who or what the story was about and where the story happened. If the story is informational, ask students what facts they remember.

Writing To reinforce letter formation, have students practice writing the letter *p* in the following fun way. Direct them to draw very large letter forms in the air using their fingers as a pencil.

Reinforcement Activities

1. Write some simple words on the board. Ask volunteers to identify and circle a specific letter (*b, f, m, k, t, r, p*) in each word.

2. Assign pairs of students a previously learned letter. Have them search the classroom for objects or pictures of objects beginning with that letter sound. Then have them share their findings with the rest of the class.

Teaching the Letter *s*

Materials: Wall Chart **sock, pear, rocket, turkey,** and other review objects; Picture–Letter Cards for *s*

Picture book suggestions: *The Reasons for Seasons* by Gail Gibbons; *Sammy the Seal* by Syd Hoff

Quick Review

Ask students to listen and tell you what letter makes the /p/ sound [*p*]. Then ask them to name the key word for the letter *p* [*pear*]. Hold up the Wall Chart **pear**. Toss the **pear** to a student as you say /p/. Tell the student to catch it and say: "*p* says /p/ as in *pear*." Throw it a few more times along with other review objects, and have different students respond each time.

Phonemic Awareness

Display the Wall Chart **sock** and ask students to name it. Have the class repeat the word *sock* several times. Then ask the class to say only the first sound in *sock* [/s/]. Have them repeat the /s/ sound.

Ask the class what sound they hear at the beginning of *sand*. Is this the same sound as at the beginning of *sock*? Then ask the class to indicate with thumbs up or thumbs down if the following words begin with /s/: *song, soup, dinner, Saturday, apple, Sunday, sat, sick, give, sun, sale, silly.*

Phonics

Introduce the Skill Say the word *sock*, emphasizing the initial consonant sound. Ask students if they can name the letter that stands for the sound /s/ that they hear at the beginning of *sock, sick, sun,* and *soccer.*

Write the letter *s* on the board or show the *s* picture–letter card. Tell the class that this is the letter *s,* and it stands for the sound at the beginning of *sock.* Hold up the Wall Chart **sock** or sock picture card. Say the letter name, the sound, and key word: "*s* says /s/ as in *sock.*" Have the class repeat the phrase.

Ask students to name other words that begin like *sock,* then ask what letter the words begin with. Clarify any incorrect responses.

Vocabulary

Introduce New Vocabulary Words from this lesson include **seat belt, scissors, sandwich, sink, sock, saw, sun,** and **sick.** Clarify the meaning of these words, as necessary, during the lesson.

Completing Student Pages 15–28

Page 15. Read the directions aloud and assist students, as necessary.

Page 16. Model formation of the letter *s* for the class. Have students write the letter in the air as you write it on the board. Have students look at the letter *s* in the middle of the page. Then have them find the number 1 and place their index fingers on it. Ask students to trace the letter, beginning at number 1 and following the stroke of that line. They should say the letter and its sound as they trace it. Point out the capital letter *S* in the bottom corner of the page. Remind students that capital letters are two spaces tall and are used to begin names and sentences. Reinforce letter formation with the writing suggestions provided for this lesson or by having students practice writing the letter on lined paper.

Page 17. Read the directions aloud. Make sure students move from left to right. Ask them to say both the word and the first sound in the word when they get to the picture.

Page 18. Read the directions aloud. For each row, make sure students are tracking from left to right. Point out that the bottom line shows capital letters.

Page 19. Read the directions aloud, pausing for students to respond to each part. As they color the sections, have them say the letter name, the sound of the letter, and the name of the pictured word. Remind students that they are looking for both lowercase and capital letters.

Page 20. Have the class point to each picture on page 21 as you name it: **scissors, sandwich, sock, sick, sun, saw, sink, seat belt**. Pause between each word, allowing students time to respond. Then read the questions below and have them follow the directions for the pictures on page 21.

1. I am thinking of something that is good to eat, especially for lunch. It is easy to take on a picnic. It is made of two pieces of bread with filling between them. What am I thinking of? [sandwich] Put your finger on the **sandwich**. What sound do you hear at the beginning of **sandwich**? Color the filling in the **sandwich**.

2. I am thinking of something soft that you put on your foot before you put your shoe on. A pair of them helps keep your feet warm. Can you find what I am thinking of? [sock] Put your finger on the **sock**. What sound do you hear at the beginning of **sock**? Color the heel and toe of the **sock**.

3. When a day is not cloudy or rainy, you can see this in the sky. It is bright, and its light helps plants grow. What shines brightly in the daytime sky? [sun] Put your finger on the **sun**. What sound does **sun** begin with? Color the **sun** and add more sunbeams.

4. When you get in the car, you must buckle up so you will be safe. What do you buckle? [seat belt] Put your finger on the **seat belt**. Say **seat belt** and the sound you hear at the beginning of it. Draw a head on the person with a **seat belt**.

5. Find something on this page that you can use to cut paper. Be careful with them! What are they called? [scissors] Put your finger on the picture of the **scissors**. What sound do you hear at the beginning of **scissors**? Draw a circle around the **scissors**.

6. You can use this tool to cut wood. It is made of steel and has a wooden handle. What is it called? [saw] Put your finger on the picture of the **saw**. What sound does **saw** begin with? Draw a box around the **saw**.

7. When you are not feeling well and must go to bed, we say you are ____ [sick]. Put your finger on the picture of the **sick** person. What sound does **sick** begin with? Color the blanket on the **sick** person's bed.

8. Now I am thinking of something you wash your hands and face in. You also brush your teeth here because it has water and a drain. What is it? [sink] Put your finger on the **sink**. What sound does **sink** begin with? Draw lots of suds in the **sink**.

Page 21. Read the directions aloud on page 20 while students listen and work.

Page 22. Read the directions aloud and assist students, as necessary.

Page 23. Read the directions aloud, pausing for students to complete each part. Give praise for slow, careful work.

Page 24–28. Read the directions aloud and assist students, as necessary. If the directions have multiple steps, pause for students to complete each task.

Building Fluency

Modeling Fluent Reading Select a read-aloud book or a poem that features words beginning with the letter *s*. Read the book or poem several times throughout the week, modeling left to right reading and appropriate expression. After you read the book, you may ask students to recall words from the story that begin with the letter *s*.

Building Comprehension

Using Language Review any new words from the lesson or read-aloud. Ask volunteers to use one of the new words in a sentence.

Prediction As you read aloud to the class, pause at various points throughout the story to ask students what they think will happen next. Confirm correct predictions as you read the rest of the story.

Writing To reinforce letter formation, have students practice writing the letter *s* in the following fun way. Lightly cover the bottom of a tray or other flat surface with sand, salt, or sugar. Have students write individual letters in the tray with their fingers, making the letters as large as possible.

Reinforcement Activities

1. Distribute letter cards, one per student. Write a letter on the board or overhead. Ask students with that letter to come to the front of the class. Ask one volunteer from that group to name the letter, and another volunteer to say the sound. Have other students name words that begin with the sound.

2. Ask students to indicate with thumbs up or thumbs down if the first sounds in each pair of words below are the same or different.
> *silly, sock*
> *pan, park*
> *button, mother*
> *rag, road*
> *sorry, sing*
> *puddle, seven*
> *ready, shout*
> *kid, kettle*
> *sun, sack*

Teaching the Letter *n*

Materials: Wall Chart **nest, pear, sock, rocket,** and other review objects; Picture–Letter
Cards for *n, s, p*

Picture book suggestion: *Night Noises* by Mem Fox, Terry Denton (illus.)

Quick Review

Display the letter *s*. Ask students to name it and tell what sound it makes [/s/]. Then ask them to name the key word that starts with *s* [*sock*]. Hold up the Wall Chart **sock** and have the class repeat: "*s* says /s/ as in *sock*." Repeat with *p, r,* and other review letters.

Phonemic Awareness

Display the Wall Chart **nest** and ask students to name it. Have the class repeat the word nest several times. Then ask the class to say only the first sound in *nest* [/n/]. Have them repeat the /n/ sound.

Ask the class what sound they hear at the beginning of *nest*. Is this the same sound they hear at the beginning of *nose*? Then ask the class to indicate with thumbs up or thumbs down if the following words begin with /n/: *neck, moose, nice, mice, next, near, hill, north, never.*

Phonics

Introduce the Skill Say the word *nest*, emphasizing the initial consonant sound. Ask students if they can name the letter that stands for the sound /n/ they hear at the beginning of *nest, nice, not,* and *nap*.

Write the letter *n* on the board or show the *n* picture–letter card. Tell the class that this is the letter *n*, and it stands for the sound at the beginning of nest. Hold up the Wall Chart **nest** or nest picture card. Say the letter name, the sound, and key word: "*n* says /n/ as in *nest*." Have the class repeat the phrase.

Ask students to name other words that begin like *nest*, then ask what letter the words begin with. Clarify any incorrect responses.

Vocabulary

Introduce New Vocabulary Words from this lesson include **nail, necktie, newspaper, net, napkin, nest, needle,** and **necklace.** Clarify the meaning of these words, as necessary.

Completing Student Pages 29–40

Page 29. Read the directions aloud and assist students, as necessary.

Page 30. Model formation of the letter *n* for the class. Have students write the letter in the air as you write it on the board. Have students look at the letter *n* in the middle of the page. Then have them find the number 1 and place their index fingers on it. Ask students to start tracing the letter, beginning at number 1 and following the stroke of the first line. To continue, have them find the number 2 and follow that line. They should say the letter and its sound as they trace it. Point out the capital letter *N* in the bottom corner of the page. Remind students that capital letters are two spaces tall and are used to begin names and sentences. Reinforce letter formation with the writing suggestions provided for this lesson or by having students practice writing the letter on lined paper.

Page 31. Read the directions aloud. Make sure students move from left to right. Ask them to say both the word and the first sound in the word when they get to the picture.

Page 32. Have the class point to each picture on page 33 as you name it: **newspaper, napkin, necklace, needle, nest, net, nail, necktie.** Pause between each word, allowing students time to respond. Then read the questions below and have them follow the directions for the pictures on page 33.

1. I am thinking of something that is used to catch butterflies and sometimes fish or crabs. It has a long handle; a hoop at the end holds a mesh bag. What is it called? [net] Put your finger on the **net**. What sound do you hear at the beginning of **net**? Color the **net** yellow.

2. I am thinking of something people read to learn about the news of the world. Sometimes it has comics in it, too. It is called a _____ [newspaper]. Put your finger on the **newspaper**. What sound do you hear at the beginning of **newspaper**? Put a big X on the **newspaper**.

3. Find something on this page that you wipe your mouth with when you are eating. Sometimes it is made of soft paper and other times it is made of cloth. What is it? [napkin] Put your finger on the **napkin**. What sound do you hear at the beginning of **napkin**? Color the **napkin** your favorite color.

4. I am thinking of something made of metal. It is thin and one end is pointed. You hammer it into two pieces of wood to hold them together. What is it? [nail] Put your finger on the **nail**. What sound does **nail** begin with? Say the sound again. Draw a box around the **nail**.

5. Men may wear one of these when they dress up or go to work. They put it around their neck and tie a knot in it. What is it? [necktie] Put your finger on the **necktie**. What sound does **necktie** begin with? Color the **necktie** red.

6. Now I am thinking of something else people wear around their necks when they dress up. Sometimes it is made of gold or beads. It can have sparkly jewels attached to it. What is it called? [necklace] Put your finger on the **necklace**. What sound do you hear at the beginning of **necklace**? Draw some more jewels on the **necklace**.

7. I am thinking of something that some birds use for their home. They can make it out of grass and weeds; then they lay their eggs in it. What is it? [nest] Put your finger on the **nest**. Say the sound at the beginning of **nest**. Color just the eggs in this **nest**.

8. The last thing is used with thread for sewing. It is long and thin. What is it called? [needle] Put your finger on the **needle**. Say **needle** and the sound you hear at the beginning of it. Draw a circle around the **needle**.

Page 33. Read the directions aloud on page 32 while students listen and work.

Page 34. Read the directions aloud. Make sure students are tracking from left to right. Point out to students that the bottom line shows capital letters.

Page 35. Read the directions aloud, pausing for students to complete each part. Give praise for slow, careful work.

Page 36–40. Read the directions aloud and assist students, as necessary. If the directions have multiple steps, pause for students to complete each task.

Building Fluency

Modeling Fluent Reading Select a read-aloud book or a poem that features words beginning with the letter *n*. Read the book or poem several times throughout the week, modeling left to right reading and appropriate expression.

Building Comprehension

Extending Word Knowledge Give students opportunities to talk about new words in different contexts. For example, ask students what kind of animal lives in a **nest**. Then ask them to name the homes of some other animals like bears, bats, or beavers.

Understanding Text After a read-aloud, reinforce understanding of the story by asking students to describe what happened in the story. Clarify order of events, as necessary. Ask students who or what the story was about and where the story happened. If the story is informational, ask students what facts they remember.

Writing

To reinforce letter formation, have students practice writing the letter *n* in the following fun way. Cut a piece of sandpaper in half and write a letter on each piece. Have students trace the letter with their index fingers.

Reinforcement Activities

1. Say the following word pairs, emphasizing the beginning sound. Ask students what beginning sound the following word pairs share. Then ask them to name the letter than makes that sound.

> *saddle, sense*
> *toad, turtle*
> *rule, real*
> *pond, pay*
> *talk, tend*
> *fuzzy, festival*
> *sort, save*
> *rope, run*
> *town, team*
> *box, bill*

2. Provide students with several picture cards of objects beginning with the sounds/letters learned thus far. Have students sort pictures according to their beginning sounds and/or letters. Then have the students check for accuracy by saying aloud the names of the pictures in each group.

Teaching the Letter *j*

Materials: Wall Chart **jack-o'-lantern, nest, sock, pear;** Picture–Letter Cards for *f, b, m, s*
Picture book suggestion: *The Name Jar* by Yangsook Choi

Quick Review

Display the letter *n*. Ask the class to name it and say what sound it makes [/n/]. Then ask students to name the key word for *n* [*nest*]. Hold up the **nest** from the Wall Chart and ask the class to repeat: "*n* says /n/ as in *nest*." Continue with the letters *p* [*pear*] and *s* [*sock*].

Phonemic Awareness

Display the Wall Chart **jack-o'-lantern** and ask students to name it. Have the class repeat the word *jack-o'-lantern* several times. Then ask the class to say only the first sound in *jack-o'-lantern* [/j/]. Have them repeat the /j/ sound.

Ask the class what sound they hear at the beginning of *juice*. Is this the same sound as at the beginning of *jack-o'-lantern*? Then ask the class to indicate with thumbs up or thumbs down if the following words begin with /j/: *jazz, keep, gas, just, jelly, cake, jungle, boot, match, joke.*

Phonics

Introduce the Skill Say the word *jack-o'-lantern,* emphasizing the initial consonant sound. Ask students if they can name the letter that stands for the sound /j/ that they hear at the beginning of *jack-o'-lantern, junk, Josh,* and *jade.*

Write the letter *j* on the board or show the *j* picture–letter card. Tell the class that this is the letter *j,* and it stands for the sound at the beginning of *jack-o'-lantern.* Hold up the Wall Chart **jack-o'-lantern** or jack-o'-lantern picture card. Say the letter name, the sound, and key word: "*j* says /j/ as in *jack-o'-lantern.*" Have the class repeat the phrase.

Ask students to name other words that begin like *jack-o'-lantern,* then ask what letter the words begin with. Clarify any incorrect responses.

Vocabulary

Introduce New Vocabulary Words from this lesson include **jump, juggle, jam, jelly, jungle gym, jack-in-the-box, jug, jack-o'-lantern, jacket.** Clarify the meaning of these words, as necessary, during the lesson.

Completing Student Pages 41–52

Page 41. Read the directions aloud and assist students, as necessary.

Page 42. Model formation of the letter *j* for the class. Have students write the letter in the air as you write it on the board. Have students look at the letter j in the middle of the page. Tell students to notice how the *j* hangs below the line. Then have them find the number 1 and place their index fingers on it. Ask students to trace the letter, beginning at number 1 and following the stroke of the first line. Then have them find the number 2 and tap their finger on the dot. They should say the letter and its sound as they trace it. Point out the capital letter *J* in the bottom corner of the page. Remind students that capital letters are two spaces tall and are used to begin names and sentences. Reinforce letter formation with the writing suggestions provided for this lesson or by having students practice writing the letter on lined paper.

Page 43. Read the directions aloud. Make sure students move from left to right. Ask them to say both the word and the first sound in the word when they get to the picture.

Page 44. Have the class point to each picture on page 45 as you name it: **jam, jack-in-the-box, jacket, jack-o'-lantern, jug, jungle gym, jump, juggle.** Pause between each word, allowing students time to respond. Then read the questions below and have them follow the directions for the pictures on page 45.

1. I am thinking of something you wear when it is cool. It covers the top half of your body and keeps you warm if you button it. What is it? [jacket] Put your finger on the **jacket.** What sound does **jacket** begin with? Color the **jacket** any way you want.

2. Find a picture of something you can do with a rope. It is fun and good exercise. It is called _____ rope [jumping]. Put your finger on the girl **jumping** rope. Do you like to **jump** rope? What sound do you hear at the beginning of **jump**? Draw some grass for the girl to **jump** on.

3. This is a pumpkin with a face carved in it for Halloween. Sometimes you put a light inside. Now it is called a _____ [jack-o'-lantern]. Put your finger on the **jack-o'-lantern**. What sound does **jack-o'-lantern** start with? Carefully color the **jack-o'-lantern**.

4. I am thinking of what you spread on toast. It is sweet and tasty and made from fruit. It comes in a jar. What do you call it? [jam, jelly] Either **jam** or **jelly** is a good answer. Put your finger on the **jam** or **jelly**. What sound do **jam** and **jelly** begin with? Draw a box around the jar of **jam**.

5. When you toss several balls in the air and keep catching them without dropping them, it is called _____ [juggling]. Put your finger on the picture for **juggle**. Have you ever tried to **juggle**? What sound does **juggling** begin with? Draw another ball for the juggler.

6. I am thinking of something found on a playground. It is fun to climb, swing from, and jump off one of these. Its name begins with the sound of /j/. What is it called? [jungle gym] Put your finger on the **jungle gym**. Say the sound you hear at the beginning of **jungle gym**. Add something to the **jungle gym**. Color it to make it look nice.

7. The next picture is of a toy that pops out of a box. Sometimes you turn a handle until the lid springs open. What do we call it? [jack-in-the-box] Put your finger on the **jack-in-the-box**. How many of you have seen a **jack-in-the-box**? They are lots of fun. What sound do you hear at the beginning of **jack-in-the-box**? Color the box, but not Jack!

8. The last picture shows a container that milk, cider, or syrup comes in. What is its name? [jug] Have you heard of a **jug**? Put your finger on the **jug**. Say **jug** and the sound you hear at the beginning of **jug**. Put an X on it.

Page 45. Read the directions aloud on page 44 while students listen and work.

Page 46. Read the directions aloud and assist students, as necessary.

Page 47. Read the directions aloud, pausing for students to complete each part. Give praise for slow, careful work.

Pages 48–52. Read the directions aloud and assist students, as necessary. If the directions have multiple steps, pause for students to complete each task. Identify pictures, as necessary.

Building Fluency

Modeling Fluent Reading Select a read-aloud book or a poem that features words beginning with the letter *j*. Read the book or poem several times throughout the week, modeling left to right reading and appropriate expression.

Building Comprehension

Using Language Review any new words from the lesson or read-aloud. Ask volunteers to use one of the new words in a sentence.

Visualization Read a new picture book to the class without showing the pictures. Explain that they should make a picture in their minds about what is happening in the story as they listen. Ask students to describe how they imagine the characters and places to look. Read the story a second time, showing the pictures. As you read, ask students to describe how the pictures were similar to or different from the pictures they had visualized.

Writing

To reinforce letter formation, have students practice writing the letter *j* in the following fun way. Using only their index fingers, have students draw a letter on the following objects: the floor, a desk, the rug, the wall, a table, a chair—the more texture to the surface the better!

Reinforcement Activities

1. Distribute one previously learned letter card to each student. Write a letter on the board. Ask students with that letter to come to the front of the class. Have one volunteer name the letter, and another volunteer say the sound. Ask other students to name words that begin with that sound.

2. Ask students to say the beginning sound that is the same in each set of words. Then have them name the letter that represents that sound.

made, man, mash
pillow, point, pass
news, nine, nurse
send, sit, soup
pet, pick, puppet
round, rose, roof
tear, tell, talk
fort, food, fig
basket, barn, bottle

Teaching the Letter *h*

Materials: Wall Chart **jack-o'-lantern, pear, sock, hat, nest;**
Picture–Letter Cards for *j, p, n, s, h*
Picture book suggestions: *Hat, Hats, Hats* by Ann Morris, Ken Heyman (illus.);
The Pigeon Finds a Hot Dog! by Mo Willems

Quick Review

Display the Wall Chart **jack-o'-lantern** and ask students to name it. Ask them what sound *jack-o'-lantern* begins with and what letter makes that sound. Write a large letter *j* on the board. Then ask the class to write some *j*s in the air with their fingers. Repeat to review other letters.

Phonemic Awareness

Display the Wall Chart **hat** and ask students to name it. Have the class repeat the word *hat* several times. Then ask the class to say only the first sound in *hat* [/h/]. Have students repeat the /h/ sound.

Ask the class what sound they hear at the beginning of *hippo*. Is this the same sound as at the beginning of *hat*? Then ask the class to indicate with thumbs up or thumbs down if the following words begin with /h/: *hamster, bunny, home, hands, neck, happy, lap, hotel, pal, how, handle.*

Phonics

Introduce the Skill Say the word *hat*, emphasizing the initial consonant sound. Ask students if they can name the letter that stands for the sound /h/ that they hear at the beginning of *hat, hello, hop, hunt.*

Write the letter *h* on the board or show the *h* picture–letter card. Tell the class that this is the letter *h*, and it stands for the sound at the beginning of *hat*. Hold up the Wall Chart **hat** or hat picture card. Say the letter name, the sound, and key word: "*h* says /h/ as in *hat.*" Have the class repeat the phrase.

Ask students to name other words that begin like *hat*, and then ask what letter the words begin with. Clarify any incorrect responses.

Vocabulary

Introduce New Vocabulary Words from this lesson include **hat, horse, hammer, hot dog, house, hangers, horn,** and **hand**. Clarify the meaning of these words, as necessary, during the lesson.

Completing Student Pages 53–66

Page 53. Read the directions aloud and assist students, as necessary.

Page 54. Model formation of the letter *h* for the class. Have students write the letter in the air as you write it on the board. Have students look at the letter *h* in the middle of the page. Then have them find the number 1 and place their index fingers on it. Ask students to start tracing the letter, beginning at number 1 and following the stroke of the first line. To continue, have them find the number 2 and follow that line. They should say the letter and its sound as they trace it. Point out the capital letter *H* in the bottom corner of the page. Remind students that capital letters are two spaces tall and are used to begin names and sentences. Reinforce letter formation with the writing suggestions provided for this lesson or by having students practice writing the letter on lined paper.

Page 55. Read the directions aloud. Make sure students move from left to right. Ask them to say both the word and the first sound in the word when they get to the picture.

Page 56. Read the directions aloud. Make sure students are tracking from left to right. Point out that the bottom line shows capital letters.

Page 57. Have students count the hats on this page. Read the directions aloud to students.

Page 58. Have the class point to each picture on page 59 as you name it: **hammer, house, hand, horn, hangers, hot dog, hat, horse.** Pause between each word, allowing students time to respond. Then read the questions below and have them follow the directions for the pictures on page 59.

1. I am thinking of something that tastes good. It has a bun around it and is fun to eat at a baseball game. What is it? [hot dog] Put your finger on the **hot dog**. What sound does **hot dog** begin with? Draw a box around the **hot dog**.

2. I am thinking of a part of your body that is attached to your arm. You use it nearly every time you do something. It has fingers and a thumb. What is it? [hand] Put your finger on the **hand**. What sound do you hear at the beginning of **hand**? Find the **hand** and draw a ring on one of the fingers.

3. I am thinking of something you hang your clothes on in a closet. It is made of wire or plastic. What is it? [hanger] Put your finger on the **hangers**. Say the sound you hear at the beginning of **hanger**. Draw an X on the hangers.

4. You can use this tool to pound nails into wood. It has a wooden handle and a metal head. What is it? [hammer] Put your finger on the **hammer**. Can you hear the /h/ sound at the beginning of **hammer**? Say it. Color the head of the **hammer**.

5. I am thinking of something people live in. It has doors, windows, a roof, and some-times a chimney. What is it? [house] Put your finger on the **house**. What sound does **house** begin with? Draw a path up to the front door and color the **house**.

6. This is something that makes a loud noise. Cars always have one. Sometimes bikes have one, too. What do you call it? [horn] Put your finger on the **horn**. Say the sound at the beginning of **horn**. Draw a circle around the **horn**.

7. Find something you can wear on your head to keep the sun or rain off. What is its name? [hat] Put your finger on the **hat**. What sound do you hear at the beginning of **hat**? Draw a person wearing this **hat**.

8. I am thinking of a big animal with four legs. It can run fast. You can sometimes ride on its back or hitch it to a wagon. What is the name of this animal? [horse] Put your finger on the **horse**. What sound does **horse** begin with? Color the **horse**.

Page 59. Read the directions aloud on page 58 while students listen and work.

Page 60. Together, identify the pictures on the page. Ask the students to say the sound of the letter shown in the box. Read the directions aloud and assist students, as necessary.

Page 61. Read the directions aloud, pausing for students to complete each part. Give praise for slow, careful work.

Pages 62–66. Read the directions aloud and assist students, as necessary. If the directions have multiple steps, pause for students to complete each task. Identify pictures, as necessary.

Building Fluency

Modeling Fluent Reading Select a read-aloud book or a poem that features words beginning with the letter *h*. Read the book or poem several times throughout the week, modeling left to right reading and appropriate expression.

Building Comprehension

Extending Word Knowledge Give students opportunities to talk about new words in different contexts. For example, remind students that a **hammer** is a special tool used for pounding nails into wood. Ask students to name some other kinds of tools and tell what they are used for.

Understanding Text After a read-aloud, reinforce understanding of the story by asking students to describe what happened in the story. Clarify order of events, as necessary. Ask students who or what the story was about and where the story happened. If the story is informational, ask students what facts they remember.

Writing

To reinforce letter formation, have students practice writing the letter *h* in the following fun way. 1) Put a small amount of shaving cream on a tray or other flat surface and have the students write letters in it. 2) Have students choose from a selection of pre-cut hats made from construction paper. They can practice writing the letter *h* on their hats. Then provide students with glue and a variety of simple decorations, to personalize their hats.

Reinforcement Activities

1. Start an I Spy game by saying: "I spy something that begins with /h/." Have the class try to guess what the object is. The student who answers correctly starts the next round in the same way with a different sound.

2. Say a word that begins with the letter *s, p, n, j,* or *h.* Ask volunteers to say the first sound in each word and name the letter that represents that sound. Possible words: *heart, penny, sea, pod, nut, jeans, sub, note, joke, puff, joy, heal, nickel, help, safe.*

Teaching the Letter *d*

Materials: Wall Chart sock, nest, jack-o'-lantern, hat, and other review objects;
Picture–Letter Cards for ***d, h, j, n, s, p***
Picture book suggestions: *The Stray Dog* by Marc Simont;
Danny and the Dinosaur by Syd Hoff

Quick Review

Display the Wall Chart **hat.** Ask students to name it and say the first sound [/h/]. Ask them what letter makes this sound. Then toss the **hat** to a student as you say /h/. Have the student who catches it say: "*h* says /h/ as in *hat.*" Throw it a few more times along with the **sock, jack-o'-lantern,** and **nest,** and have different students respond each time. Incorporate other review objects.

Phonemic Awareness

Display the Wall Chart **duck** and ask students to name it. Have the class repeat the word *duck* several times. Then ask the class to say only the first sound in *duck* [/d/]. Have them repeat the /d/ sound.

    Ask the class what sound they hear at the beginning of *dirt.* Is this the same sound as at the beginning of *duck*? Ask them to tell you which of the following words begins with /d/: *damp, camp, dinner, disk, tiger, dip, sank, dust, march, dish.*

Phonics

Introduce the Skill Say the word *duck*, emphasizing the initial consonant sound. Ask students if they can name the letter that stands for the sound /d/ that they hear at the beginning of *duck, dip, dock,* and *dent.*

Write the letter *d* on the board or show the *d* picture–letter card. Tell the class that this is the letter *d*, and it stands for the sound at the beginning of *duck*. Hold up the Wall Chart **duck** or duck picture card. Say the letter name, the sound, and key word: "*d* says /d/ as in *duck*," Have the class repeat the phrase.

Ask students to name other words that begin like *duck*, and then ask what letter the words begin with. Clarify any incorrect responses.

Vocabulary

Introduce New Vocabulary Words from this lesson include **doll, duck, dice, dog, dinosaur, dish, dive,** and **dig**. Clarify the meaning of these words, as necessary, during the lesson.

Completing Student Pages 67–78

Page 67. Read the directions aloud and assist students, as necessary.

Page 68. Model formation of the letter *d* for the class. Have students write the letter in the air as you write it on the board. Have students look at the letter *d* in the middle of the page. Then have them find the number 1 and place their index fingers on it. Ask students to start tracing the letter, beginning at number 1 and following the stroke of the first line. To continue, have them find the number 2 and follow that line. They should say the letter and its sound as they trace it. Point out the capital letter *D* in the bottom corner of the page. Remind students that capital letters are two spaces tall and are used to begin names and sentences. Reinforce letter formation with the writing suggestions provided for this lesson or by having students practice writing the letter on lined paper.

Page 69. Read the directions aloud. Make sure students move from left to right. Ask them to say both the word and the first sound in the word when they get to the picture.

Page 70. Have the class point to each picture on page 71 as you name it: **dice, duck, dinosaur, dig, dive, dish, dog, doll.** Pause between each word, allowing students time to respond. Then read the questions below and have them follow the directions for the pictures on page 71.

1. I am thinking of an animal that makes a quacking sound. It can swim on a pond. What is it? [duck] Put your finger on the **duck**. What sound does **duck** begin with? Color the water blue and the **duck** any color you wish.

2. I am thinking of an animal that is playful and fun. It wags its tail when it likes you. Sometimes it barks. What is it called? [dog] Put your finger on the **dog**. Say the sound at the beginning of **dog**. Draw a leash on the **dog**.

3. I am thinking of something that lived a long time ago. It was very large. This pre-historic animal was one of the first creatures on earth. What is it? [dinosaur] Put your finger on the **dinosaur**. Say the sound at the beginning of **dinosaur**. Draw a box around the **dinosaur**.

4. I am thinking of a toy that looks like a baby but is not real. It is fun to play with. You can dress it up in clothes. What is it called? [doll] Put your finger on the **doll**. What sound does **doll** begin with? Color the **doll** any way you like.

5. Find something you might use to play board games. You shake them and throw them down so you can count the dots on top. What are these called? [dice] Put your finger on the **dice**. Have you ever seen **dice**? What sound does **dice** start with? Draw a circle around the **dice**.

6. If you jump off a high board with your arms out straight and go head first into the water, it is called a ____ [dive]. Put your finger on the picture of the person **diving**. Learning to **dive** takes a lot of practice in deep water. Say the sound you hear at the beginning of **dive**. Color the water blue or green.

7. I am thinking of something you put food on. When you finish eating from it, you must wash the _____ [dish]. Put your finger on the **dish**. What sound do you hear at the beginning of **dish**? Draw some food in the **dish**.

8. The last picture shows a girl making deep holes in the ground with a shovel. What is she doing? [digging] Put your finger on the picture of the girl **digging**. What sound does **dig** begin with? Draw an X on the girl who is **digging**.

Page 71. Read the directions aloud on page 70 while students listen and work.

Page 72. Read the directions aloud and assist students, as necessary.

Page 73. Read the directions aloud, pausing for students to complete each part. Give praise for slow, careful work.

Pages 74–78. Read the directions aloud and assist students, as necessary. If the directions have multiple steps, pause for students to complete each task. Identify pictures, as necessary.

Building Fluency

Modeling Fluent Reading Select a read-aloud book or a poem that features words beginning with the letter *d*. Read the book or poem several times throughout the week, modeling left to right reading and appropriate expression. After you read the book, you may ask students to recall words from the story that begin with the letter *d*.

Building Comprehension

Using Language Review any new words from the lesson or read-aloud. Ask volunteers to use one of the new words in a sentence.

Prediction As you read aloud to the class, pause at various points throughout the story to ask students what they think will happen next. Confirm correct predictions as you read the rest of the story.

Writing

To reinforce letter formation, have students practice writing the letter *d* in the following fun way. Provide a straw mat, a small rag rug, or a piece of screening, and have students write letters on it with their index fingers.

Reinforcement Activities

1. Play Pick a Picture. Place the *d, h, j, n, s, p* picture cards along the front of the board. Then say a word, such as *pumpkin*, and call on a student. Have the student go to the board and point to the picture beginning with the same sound as *pumpkin* [pear]. Continue with other words until all students have had a turn.

2. Working with letters learned in Books A and B, provide students with a card set of lowercase letters and a card set of capital letters. Have students match each lowercase letter with its corresponding capital letter.

For additional reinforcement, play some of the games described in the *Explode The Code Wall Chart Activity Book*. Playing short games at different times of the day helps reinforce learning and make it fun. This activity book describes thirty-five different games that can be played using the Wall Chart objects.

Go for The Code
Book C

Teaching the Letter *c*

Materials: Wall Chart: cake, duck, hat, jack-o'-lantern, and other review objects;
Picture–Letter Cards for *c*
Picture book suggestions: *The Caterpillar and the Polliwog* **by Jack Kent;**
Click, Clack, Moo: Cows that Type **by Doreen Cronin, Betsy Lewin (illus.)**

Quick Review

Display the Wall Chart **duck**. Have students name it and say the first sound [/d/]. Ask them what letter makes this sound. Then toss the **duck** to a student as you say /d/. Have the student who catches it say: "d says /d/ as in *duck*." Throw it a few more times along with the **hat** and **jack-o'-lantern**, and have different students respond each time. Incorporate other review objects.

Phonemic Awareness

Display the Wall Chart **cake** and ask students to name it. Have the class repeat the word *cake* several times. Then ask the class to say only the first sound in *cake* [/k/]. Have students repeat the /k/ sound.

Ask the class what sound they hear at the beginning of *coat*. Is this the same sound as at the beginning of *cake*? Then ask the class to tell you if the following words begin with /k/: *cub, fun, cover, cook, bear, rate, have, cool, cold, join, dime, card, coal.*

Phonics

Introduce the Skill Say the word *cake*, emphasizing the initial consonant sound. Ask students if they can name the letter that stands for the sound /k/ they hear at the beginning of *cake, cot, cat, care,* and *can.* Remind students that there is another letter they already learned that makes the /k/ sound. Ask them to name that letter [k]. Tell them that in this lesson they will be working with /k/ words that begin with the letter *c*.

Write the letter *c* on the board or show the *c* picture–letter card. Tell the class that this is the letter *c*, and it stands for the sound they hear at the beginning of *cake*. Hold up the Wall Chart **cake** or cake picture card. Say the letter name, the sound, and key word: "c says /k/ as in *cake*." Have the class repeat the phrase.

Ask students to name other words that begin like *cake*, and then ask what letter the words begin with. Clarify any incorrect responses.

Vocabulary

Introduce New Vocabulary Words from this lesson include **cup, cake, cat, candle, car, carrot, comb,** and **cow.** Clarify the meaning of these words, as necessary, during the lesson.

Review Direction Words In this and subsequent lessons, students are asked to: color objects; trace, copy, and write letters; follow a path with a pencil; circle letters; draw objects; work with colors; identify numbers 1, 2, and 3; and understand meanings of *same/different*, *below*, and *left/right*. Review the directions with the class, as necessary, before beginning each exercise.

Completing Student Pages 1–14

Page 1. Read the directions aloud and assist students, as necessary.

Page 2. Model formation of the letter *c* for the class. Have students write the letter in the air as you write it on the board. Have students look at the letter *c* in the middle of the page. Then have them find the number 1 and place their index fingers on it. Ask students to trace the letter, beginning at number 1 and following the stroke of that line. Have students say the letter and its sound as they trace it. Point out the capital letter *C* in the bottom corner of the page. Tell students that capital letters are two spaces tall and are used to begin names and sentences. Reinforce letter formation with the writing suggestions provided for this lesson or by having students practice writing the letter on lined paper.

Page 3. Read the directions aloud. Make sure students move from left to right. Ask them to say both the word and the first sound in the word when they get to the picture.

Page 4. Read the directions aloud, pausing for students to respond. As they color each section, they should say the letter name, the sound of the letter, and the name of the pictured word. Remind them that they are looking for both lowercase and capital letters.

Page 5. Read the directions aloud. For each row, make sure students are tracking from left to right. Point out that the bottom line shows capital letters.

Page 6. Have the class point to each picture on page 7 as you name it: **cup, cake, cat, candle, car, carrot, comb, cow.** Pause between each word, allowing students time to respond. Then read the questions below and have them follow the directions for the pictures on page 7.

1. I am thinking of a dessert that is sweet and delicious. It is covered with frosting and sometimes we put candles on it. What is it? [cake] Put your finger on the **cake**. What sound do you hear at the beginning of **cake**? Color the **cake** any way you wish.

2. I am thinking of something that has to be lighted. Its flame glows and gives off light. What is it? [candle] Put your finger on the **candle**. What sound does **candle** begin with? Say the sound. Give the **candle** some smoke.

3. Find something on this page that you can use to make your hair neat. It is flat and has teeth. When you pull it through your hair, it takes the tangles out. What is it? [comb] Put your finger on the **comb**. What sound does **comb** begin with? Draw a circle around the **comb**.

4. I am thinking of an animal that makes the milk we drink. Can you say the sound this animal makes? What is this animal called? [cow] Put your finger on the **cow**. What sound does **cow** begin with? Say the sound again. Color the horns and spots on the **cow**.

5. I am thinking of a vegetable that is orange. You can eat it raw for a snack. Rabbits like to eat it, too. What is this vegetable called? [carrot] Put your finger on the **carrot**. What sound does **carrot** begin with? Color the **carrot** orange.

6. I am thinking of something you can drink from. Sometimes it sits on a saucer. What is it? [cup] Put your finger on the **cup**. Say the sound that **cup** begins with. Draw a box around the **cup**.

7. I am thinking of something that you ride in. It has four wheels and a motor, and it needs gas to run. What is it? [car] Put your finger on the **car**. What sound does **car** begin with? Say the sound again. Draw a road for the **car** to drive on.

8. That last picture is of a lovable animal. It is soft and furry and says meow. What is it? [cat] Put your finger on the **cat**. What sound does **cat** begin with? Carefully color the **cat**.

Page 7. Read the directions aloud on page 6 while students listen and work.

Page 8. Read the directions aloud and assist students, as necessary.

Page 9. Read the directions aloud, pausing for students to complete each part. Give praise for slow, careful work.

Page 10–14. Read the directions aloud and assist students, as necessary. If the directions have multiple steps, pause for students to complete each task. Identify pictures, as necessary.

Building Fluency

Modeling Fluent Reading   Select a read-aloud book or a poem that features words beginning with the letter *c*. Read the book or poem several times throughout the week, modeling left to right reading and appropriate expression.

Building Comprehension

Extending Word Knowledge Give students opportunities to talk about new words in different contexts. For example, ask students if a **carrot** is a fruit or a vegetable. Have students name as many other vegetables as they can. Also, talk to students about how the word **comb** describes both an object (a **comb** that you use to make your hair neat) and an action (you **comb** your hair).

Understanding Text After a read-aloud, reinforce understanding of the story by asking students to describe what happened in the story. Clarify order of events, as necessary. Ask students who or what the story was about and where the story happened. If the story is informational, ask students what facts they remember.

Writing

To reinforce letter formation, have students practice writing the letter *c* in the following fun way. Provide whiteboards for each student and have them write the letter as large as possible with the marker provided. Then have all students display their boards at the same time to show the accuracy of their letters. Repeat with other letters previously learned.

Reinforcement Activities

1. Start an I Spy game by saying: "I spy something that begins with /k/." Have the class try to guess what the object is. The student who answers correctly starts the next round in the same way with a different sound.

2. Have students say the sound they hear at the **end** of each word. Then ask them to name the letter that represents that sound. As necessary, start by segmenting the individual phonemes in each word so the students can hear each sound: /s/ /i/ /t/. Then ask them to say the last sound they heard. Use the following examples: *sit, pan, leaf, gas, red, top, kid, gum, cub, if, deep.*

Teaching the Letter *l*

Materials: Wall Chart leaf, duck, hat, jack-o'-lantern, and other review objects;
Picture–Letter Cards for *l*
Picture book suggestions: *Leo the Late Bloomer* **by Robert Kraus,** *Jose Aruego* **(illus.);**
Lyle, Lyle, Crocodile **by Bernard Waber**

Quick Review

Display the letter *c.* Ask the class to name it and tell what sound it makes [/k/]. Then ask them to name the key word for *c* [*cake*]. Hold up the **cake** from the Wall Chart and ask the class to repeat: "*c* says /k/ as in *cake*." Repeat with other review letters.

Phonemic Awareness

Display the Wall Chart **leaf** and ask students to name it. Have the class repeat the word *leaf* several times. Then ask the class to say only the first sound in *leaf* [/l/]. Have students repeat the /l/ sound.

Ask the class what sound they hear at the beginning of *lion*. Is this the same sound as at the beginning of *leaf*? Then ask the class to tell you if the following words begin with /l/: *lip, last, jump, love, lamb, last, life, rock, letter, hush, lift, lesson.*

Phonics

Introduce the Skill Say the word *leaf*, emphasizing the initial consonant sound. Ask students if they can name the letter that stands for the sound /l/ that they hear at the beginning of *leaf, lip,* and *late.*

Write the letter *l* on the board or show the *l* picture–letter card. Tell the class that this is the letter *l*, and it stands for the sound at the beginning of *leaf*. Hold up the Wall Chart **leaf** or leaf picture card. Say the letter name, the sound, and key word: "*l* says /l/ as in *leaf*." Have the class repeat the phrase.

Ask students to name other words that begin like *leaf*, and then ask what letter the words begin with. Clarify any incorrect responses.

Vocabulary

Introduce New Vocabulary Words from this lesson include **leaf, lamp, lips, lion, ladder, leg, letter,** and **lightbulb**. Clarify the meaning of these words, as necessary, during the lesson.

Completing Student Pages 15–28

Page 15. Read the directions aloud and assist students, as necessary.

Page 16. Model formation of the letter *l* for the class. Have students write the letter in the air as you write it on the board. Have students look at the letter *l* in the middle of the page. Then have them find the number 1 and place their index fingers on it. Ask students to trace the letter, beginning at number 1 and following the stroke of the line. Have students say the letter and its sound as they trace it. Point out the capital letter *L* in the bottom corner of the page. Remind students that capital letters are two spaces tall and are used to begin names and sentences. Reinforce letter formation with the writing suggestions provided for this lesson or by having students practice writing the letter on lined paper.

Page 17. Read the directions aloud. Make sure students move from left to right. Ask them to say both the word and the first sound in the word when they get to the picture.

Page 18. Read the directions aloud and assist students, as necessary.

Page 19. Read the directions aloud. For each row, make sure students are tracking from left to right. Point out to students that the bottom line shows capital letters.

Page 20. Have the class point to each picture on page 21 as you name it: **leaf, lips, ladder, lightbulb, letter, lion, leg, lamp.** Pause between each word, allowing students time to respond. Then read the questions below and have them follow the directions for the pictures on page 21.

1. I am thinking of something that is sent in the mail. A person writes a message on paper and puts it in an envelope with a stamp on it. What am I thinking of? [letter] Put your finger on the **letter**. What sound do you hear at the beginning of **letter**? Draw an X on the **letter**.

2. I am thinking of something green that grows on a tree or bush. Sometimes it turns red or yellow in the fall and drops off. What is it? [leaf] Put your finger on the **leaf**. Can you hear /l/ at the beginning of **leaf**? Say /l/, and color the **leaf** green, red, or yellow.

3. Find something on this page that you might use to climb up high in a tree or on a roof. It has rungs to put your feet on as you climb. What is it called? [ladder] Put your finger on the **ladder**. What sound does **ladder** begin with? Draw a circle around the **ladder**.

4. I am thinking of a very large wild animal that has a mane and roars. What is its name? [lion] Put your finger on the **lion**. Say the sound you hear at the beginning of **lion**. Draw a piece of meat for the **lion** to eat.

5. I am thinking of a part of the body. You have two of them and they help you walk. You wear pants to cover them and keep them warm. What are they? [legs] Put your finger on the **leg**. What sound do you hear at the beginning of **leg**? Draw a box around the **leg**.

6. This object gives off light when you turn it on. Sometimes it has a shade to cover it. What is it called? [lamp] Put your finger on the picture of the **lamp**. What sound does **lamp** begin with? Color the **lamp**shade any color you wish.

7. Now find a picture of a part of a face. You lick these with your tongue when you eat something tasty. They help you talk. When the weather is cold, they might get chapped and sting. What are they called? [lips] Put your finger on the picture of the **lips**. What sound do you hear at the beginning of **lips**? Say the sound. Draw a face around the **lips**.

8. The last picture is of the part of a lamp that gives off light. You can turn it on and off by a switch. What is it? [lightbulb] Put your finger on the picture of the **lightbulb**. Say the sound at the beginning of **lightbulb**. Color the **lightbulb** yellow.

Page 21. Read the directions aloud on page 20 while students listen and work.

Page 22. Read the directions aloud and assist students, as necessary.

Page 23. Read the directions aloud, pausing for students to complete each part. Give praise for slow, careful work.

Page 24–28. Read the directions aloud and assist students, as necessary. If the directions have multiple steps, pause for students to complete each task. Identify pictures, as necessary.

Building Fluency

Modeling Fluent Reading Select a read-aloud book or a poem that features words beginning with the letter *l*. Read the book or poem several times throughout the week, modeling left to right reading and appropriate expression.

Building Comprehension

Using Language Review any new words from the lesson or read-aloud. Ask volunteers to use one of the new words in a sentence.

Prediction As you read aloud to the class, pause at various points throughout the story to ask students what they think will happen next. Confirm correct predictions as you read the rest of the story.

Writing

To reinforce letter formation, have students practice writing the letter *l* in the following fun way. Have the class write very large letter forms in the air using their fingers as a pencil.

Reinforcement Activities

1. Ask students to tell you if they hear the /l/ sound at the beginning or end of each word you say. Use the following examples: *land, lunch, bowl, long, loaf, cool, lick, feel, hill.* As necessary, segment or stretch out the individual sounds in each word as you say it.

2. Distribute one letter card of a previously learned letter to each student. Write a letter on the board. Ask students with that letter to come to the front of the class. Have one volunteer from that group name the letter, and another volunteer say the sound. Ask other students to name words that begin with that sound.

Teaching the Letter *g*

Materials: Wall Chart **goat, duck, leaf, cake,** and other review objects;
Picture–Letter Cards for *g*
Picture book suggestions: *Whose Garden Is It?* by Mary Ann Hoberman, Jane Dyer (illus.);
Three Billy Goats Gruff by Mary Finch, Roberta Arenson, Peter Christen Asbjornsen (illus.)

Quick Review

Ask students to listen and tell you what letter makes the /l/ sound [*l*]. Then have them name the key word for the letter *l* [*leaf*]. Hold up the Wall Chart **leaf**. Toss it to a student as you say /l/. Have the student who catches it say: "*l* says /l/ as in *leaf*." Throw it a few more times along with other review objects, and have different students respond each time.

Phonemic Awareness

Display the Wall Chart **goat** and ask students to name it. Have the class repeat the word *goat* several times. Then ask the class to say only the first sound in goat [/g/]. Have students repeat the /g/ sound.

Ask the class what sound they hear at the beginning of *give*. Is this the same sound as at the beginning of *goat*? Then ask the class to tell you if the following words begin with /g/: *girl, hop, game, good, give, peek, goose, kind, jet, gust, gift.*

Phonics

Introduce the Skill Say the word *goat*, emphasizing the initial consonant sound. Ask students if they can name the letter that stands for the sound /g/ that they hear at the beginning of *goat, gave, girl,* and *go*.

Write the letter *g* on the board or show the *g* picture–letter card. Tell the class that this is the letter *g*, and it stands for the sound at the beginning of *goat*. Hold up the Wall Chart **goat** or goat picture card. Say the letter name, the sound, and key word: "*g* says /g/ as in *goat*." Then have the class repeat the phrase.

Ask students to name other words that begin like *goat*, and then ask what letter the words begin with. Clarify any incorrect responses.

Vocabulary

Introduce New Vocabulary Words from this lesson include **garden, guitar, gate, gas, golf, garage, girl,** and **goat**. Clarify the meaning of these words, as necessary, during the lesson.

Completing Student Pages 29–42

Page 29. Read the directions aloud and assist students, as necessary.

Page 30. Model formation of the letter *g* for the class. Have students write the letter in the air as you write it on the board. Have students look at the letter *g* in the middle of the page. Tell them to notice how *g* hangs below the line. Then have them find the number 1 and place their index fingers on it. Ask students to start tracing the letter, beginning at number 1 and following the stroke of the first line. To continue, have them find the number 2 and follow that line. They should say the letter and its sound as they trace it. Point out the capital letter *G* in the bottom corner of the page. Remind students that capital letters are two spaces tall and are used to begin names and sentences. Reinforce letter formation with the writing suggestions provided for this lesson or by having students practice writing the letter on lined paper.

Page 31. Read the directions aloud. Make sure students move from left to right. Ask them to say both the word and the first sound in the word when they get to the picture.

Page 32. Read the directions aloud and assist students, as necessary.

Page 33. Read the directions aloud. Make sure students are tracking from left to right. Point out to students that the bottom line shows capital letters.

Page 34. Have the class point to each picture on page 35 as you name it: **guitar, gate, golf, goat, girl, garage, gas, garden.** Pause between each word, allowing students time to respond. Then read the questions below and have them follow the directions for the pictures on page 35.

1. I am thinking of something you pump into a car at the self-service station. It makes the car go. What is it called? [gas] Put your finger on the picture for **gas**. What sound does **gas** begin with? Draw a circle around the **gas** pump.

2. I am thinking of a medium-sized animal that is sure-footed, has small horns, and eats almost anything that it finds. What animal am I thinking of? [goat] Put your finger on the **goat**. What sound do you hear at the beginning of **goat**? Draw some grass for the **goat** to nibble on.

3. I am thinking of a sport that some grown-ups think is fun to play. They use clubs to hit a small ball into a hole. What is this sport called? [golf] Put your finger on the picture of **golf**. What sound do you hear at the beginning of **golf**? Draw another ball next to the hole.

4. Find the picture on this page that shows a musical instrument. You play it by plucking the strings with your fingers or by strumming it. It makes a nice, mellow sound. What is it called? [guitar] Put your finger on the **guitar**. Say **guitar** and the sound you hear at the beginning of it. Color the **guitar** any way you wish.

5. You can keep a car inside this building. The car is driven in slowly, the big doors are closed, and then they are locked. What do we call a building you can keep a car in?

[garage] Put your finger on the **garage**. What sound does **garage** begin with? Color the **garage**, but not the car.

6. Now I am thinking of a place to grow vegetables or flowers. This is where you plant the seeds and watch as new plants grow. You have to pull out weeds. What do you call this place? [garden] Put your finger on the **garden**. What sound do you hear at the beginning of **garden**? Say it aloud. Draw another flower in this **garden**.

7. Find a picture of a young person. When she grows up she will be a woman. What is she called now? [girl] Put your finger on the **girl**. What sound does **girl** begin with? Draw a hat on the **girl**.

8. I am thinking of something that you must open to get through a fence or a wall. Sometimes you have to lift a latch to open it. What is it? [gate] Put your finger on the **gate**. What sound do you hear at the beginning of **gate**? Color the **gate** red.

Page 35. Read the directions aloud on page 34 while students listen and work.

Page 36. Read the directions aloud and assist students, as necessary.

Page 37. Read the directions aloud, pausing for students to complete each part. Give praise for slow, careful work.

Pages 38–42. Read the directions aloud and assist students, as necessary. If the directions have multiple steps, pause for students to complete each task. Identify pictures, as necessary.

Building Fluency

Modeling Fluent Reading Select a read-aloud book or a poem that features words beginning with the letter *g*. Read the book or poem several times throughout the week, modeling left to right reading and appropriate expression. After you read the book, you may ask students to recall words from the story that begin with the letter *g*.

Building Comprehension

Extending Word Knowledge Give students opportunities to talk about new words in different contexts. For example, have students talk to a partner about what might grow in a **garden**, or what kinds of tools one might use in a **garden**.

Understanding Text After a read-aloud, reinforce understanding of the story by asking students to describe what happened in the story. Clarify order of events, as necessary. Ask students who or what the story was about and where the story happened. If the story is informational, ask students what facts they remember.

Writing To reinforce letter formation, have students practice writing the letter *g* in the following fun way. Lightly cover the bottom of a tray or other flat surface with sand, salt, or sugar. Have students write individual letters in the tray with their index fingers, making the letters as large as possible.

Reinforcement Activities

1. Provide students with several picture cards of objects beginning with the sounds/letters learned thus far. Have students sort pictures according to their beginning sounds and/or letters. Then have the students check for accuracy by naming the pictures in each group.

2. Tell students you are going to name some words that **end** with the /g/ sound. Ask volunteers to provide rhyming words for each word you say. Provide examples, as necessary.

    rig [pig, wig, dig, big]

    lag [bag, sag, rag, tag, wag]

    tug [rug, bug, jug, hug]

Teaching the Letter *w*

Materials: Wall Chart **wagon, goat, cake, leaf,** and other review objects;
Picture–Letter Cards for *w*
Picture book suggestions: *Whistle for Willie* by Ezra Jack Keats;
Wind Blew by Pat Hutchins; *Feel the Wind* by Arthur Dorros;
Wiggling Worms at Work by Wendy Pfeffer, Steve Jenkins (illus.)

Quick Review

Display the Wall Chart **goat** and ask students to name it. Have them say the first sound [/g/], and ask what letter makes this sound [g]. Toss the **goat** to a student as you say /g/. Have the student who catches it say: "g says /g/ as in *goat*." Throw it a few more times along with other review objects, and have different students respond each time.

Phonemic Awareness

Display the Wall Chart **wagon** and ask students to name it. Have the class repeat the word *wagon* several times. Then ask the class to say only the first sound in wagon [/w/]. Have students repeat the /w/ sound.

    Ask the class what sound they hear at the beginning of *wish*. Is this the same sound as at the beginning of *wagon*? Then ask the class to tell you if the following words begin with /w/: *will, rest, wax, win, sock, work, wasp, keep, winter, jello, watch, wind.*

Phonics

Introduce the Skill Say the word *wagon*, emphasizing the initial consonant sound. Ask students if they can name the letter that stands for the sound /w/ that they hear at the beginning of *wagon, will, wax, work,* and *wake.*

Write the letter *w* on the board or show the *w* picture–letter card. Tell the class that this is the letter *w,* and it stands for the sound at the beginning of *wagon.* Hold up the Wall Chart **wagon** or wagon picture card. Say the letter name, the sound, and key word: "*w* says /w/ as in *wagon.*" Then have the class repeat the phrase.

Ask students to name other words that begin like *wagon,* and then ask what letter the words begin with. Clarify any incorrect responses.

Vocabulary

Introduce New Vocabulary Words from this lesson include **worm, wastebasket, watch, wink, web, wagon,** and **windmill.** Clarify the meaning of these words, as necessary, during the lesson.

Completing Student Pages 43–52

Page 43. Read the directions aloud and assist students, as necessary.

Page 44. Model formation of the letter *w* for the class. Have students write the letter in the air as you write it on the board. Have students look at the letter *w* in the middle of the page. Then have them find the number 1 and place their index fingers on it. Ask students to start tracing the letter, beginning at number 1 and following the stroke of the first line. To continue, have them find the number 2 and follow that line. They should say the letter and its sound as they trace it. Point out the capital letter *W* in the bottom corner of the page. Remind students that capital letters are two spaces tall and are used to begin names and sentences. Reinforce letter formation with the writing suggestions provided for this lesson or by having students practice writing the letter on lined paper.

Page 45. Read the directions aloud and assist students, as necessary.

Page 46. Have the class point to each picture on page 47 as you name it: **worm, wastebasket, wink, windmill, wagon, web, watch.** Pause between each word, allowing students time to respond. Then read the questions below and have them follow the directions for the pictures on page 47.

1. I am thinking of something you wear on your wrist so you know the time. What is it? [watch] Put your finger on the **watch.** What sound does **watch** begin with? Draw a box around the **watch.**

2. This is something you can do with your eyes. When you flick one eyelid closed, it is called a _____ [wink]. Put your finger on the picture of the person **winking.** What

sound do you hear at the beginning of **wink**? Draw a hat on the head of the person who is **winking**.

3. I am thinking of something that has four wheels and a long handle. You can haul things in it when you pull it behind you. What is it? [wagon] Put your finger on the **wagon**. What sound does **wagon** begin with? Color the **wagon** red.

4. I am thinking of something spiders spin. It helps them catch insects for food. What is it? [web] Put your finger on the **web**. What sound does **web** begin with? Draw a circle around the **web**.

5. The apple has something in it. What is it? [worm] Put your finger on the **worm**. You wouldn't want to eat the worm. What sound does **worm** begin with? Color the **worm**.

6. I am thinking of something that you throw waste paper into. There is at least one of these in every classroom. You dump the pencil sharpener dust into it and throw old papers in it when you clean out your desk. What is it? [wastebasket] Put your finger on the **wastebasket**. What sound does **wastebasket** begin with? Draw an X on the **wastebasket**.

7. The last picture shows a machine that works when the wind blows. It can pump water. What is it called? [windmill] Put your finger on the **windmill**. What sound does **windmill** begin with? Carefully color the **windmill** any way you like.

Page 47. Read the directions aloud on page 46 while students listen and work.

Page 48. Read the directions aloud and assist students, as necessary.

Page 49. Read the directions aloud, pausing for students to complete each part. Give praise for slow, careful work.

Pages 50–52. Read the directions aloud and assist students, as necessary. If the directions have multiple steps, pause for students to complete each task. Identify pictures, as necessary.

Building Fluency

Modeling Fluent Reading Select a read-aloud book or a poem that features words beginning with the letter *w*. Read the book or poem several times throughout the week, modeling left to right reading and appropriate expression.

Building Comprehension

Using Language Review any new words from the lesson or read-aloud. Ask volunteers to use one of the new words in a sentence.

Visualization Read a new picture book to the class without showing the pictures. Explain that they should make a picture in their minds about what is happening in the story as they listen. Ask students to describe how they imagine the characters and places to look. Read the story a second time, showing the pictures. As you read, ask students to describe how the pictures were similar to or different from the pictures they had visualized.

Writing

To reinforce letter formation, have students practice writing the letter *w* in the following fun way. Cut a piece of sandpaper in half and draw a letter on each piece. Have students trace the letter with their finger.

Reinforcement Activity

1. Say a word that begins with *l, g,* or *w.* Ask a volunteer to say the first sound of the word. Then have them come to the board and write the letter that represents that sound. Possible words: *last, gold, lemon, wake, west, get, list, wild, wolf, life, word, lion, go.*

2. Provide students with lined paper. Write a capital letter [P, S, N, J, H, D, C, L, G, or W] on the board. Have students name the letter then write the lowercase version of that same letter on their paper. For each letter they write, remind them to think about how many spaces tall the letter is or if it hangs below the line.

Teaching the Letter *y*

Materials: Wall Chart **yarn, wagon, goat, leaf,** and other review objects;
Picture–Letter Cards for *y*
Picture book suggestions: *Yo! Yes?* by Chris Raschka

Quick Review

Display the letter *w* and have students name it. Ask them what sound the letter makes [/w/]. Then ask the students to name the key word that starts with the sound /w/ [*wagon*]. Hold up the Wall Chart **wagon** and ask the class to say: "*w* says /w/ as in *wagon*." Repeat with *g, l,* and other review letters until all students have had a turn.

Phonemic Awareness

Display the Wall Chart **yarn** and ask students to name it. Have the class repeat the word *yarn* several times. Then ask the class to say only the first sound in yarn [/y/]. Have students repeat the /y/ sound.

Ask the class what sound they hear at the beginning of *yes.* Is this the same sound as at the beginning of *yarn*? Then ask the class to tell you if the following words begin with /y/: *yet, girl, young, yawn, yodel, rock, laugh, yak, yellow, wand, your.*

Phonics

Introduce the Skill   Say the word *yarn*, emphasizing the initial consonant sound. Ask students if they can name the letter that stands for the sound /y/ that they hear at the beginning of *yarn, yes, yet,* and *yawn.*

Write the letter *y* on the board or show the *y* picture–letter card. Tell the class that this is the letter *y,* and it stands for the sound at the beginning of *yarn.* Hold up the Wall Chart **yarn** or yarn picture card. Say the letter name, the sound, and key word: "*y* says /y/ as in *yarn.*" Then have the class repeat the phrase.

Ask students to name other words that begin like *yarn*, and then ask what letter the words begin with. Clarify any incorrect responses.

Vocabulary

Introduce New Vocabulary Words from this lesson include **yawn, yell, yarn,** and **yo-yo.** Clarify the meaning of these words, as necessary, during the lesson.

Completing Student Pages 53–62

Page 53. Model formation of the letter *y* for the class. Have students write the letter in the air as you write it on the board. Have students look at the letter *y* in the middle of the page. Tell them to notice how *y* hangs below the line. Then have them find the number 1 and place their index fingers on it. Ask students to start tracing the letter, beginning at number 1 and following the stroke of the first line. To continue, have them find the number 2 and follow that line. They should say the letter and its sound as they trace it. Point out the capital letter *Y* in the bottom corner of the page. Remind students that capital letters are two spaces tall and are used to begin names and sentences. Reinforce letter formation with the writing suggestions provided for this lesson or by having students practice writing the letter on lined paper.

Page 54. Read the directions aloud. Make sure students move from left to right. Ask them to say both the word and the first sound in the word when they get to the picture.

Page 55. Read the directions aloud and assist students, as necessary.

Page 56. Have the class point to each picture on page 57 as you name it: **yawn, yo-yo, yarn, yell**. Pause between each word, allowing students time to respond. Then read the questions below and have them follow the directions for the pictures on page 57.

1. I am thinking of something that you do when you are sleepy or bored. Your mouth opens wide and you _____ [yawn; Note: act this out]. Put your finger on the picture for **yawn**. What sound do you hear at the beginning of **yawn**? Draw a circle around the person who is **yawning**.

2. Sometimes when you want to get someone's attention, you do this with your voice. What word means the same as "shout loudly"? (It rhymes with bell.) [yell] Put your finger on the picture for **yell**. What sound does **yell** begin with? Draw an X on the picture of the person who is **yelling**.

3. I am thinking of a toy on a string. You put the string around your finger and make the round object move up and down. What is it? [yo-yo] Put your finger on the **yo-yo**. What sound do you hear at the beginning of **yo-yo**? Say the sound again. Color the **yo-yo** the color you like best.

4. The last picture shows something soft and very long. When people knit, they put this on the knitting needles and weave it back and forth. What is this material called? [yarn] Put your finger on the **yarn**. What sound does **yarn** begin with? Color the **yarn** the same color as a shirt or sweater you have.

Page 57. Read the directions aloud on page 56 while students listen and work.

Page 58. Read the directions aloud and assist students, as necessary.

Page 59. Read the directions aloud, pausing for students to complete each part. Give praise for slow, careful work.

Pages 60–62. Read the directions aloud and assist students, as necessary. If the directions have multiple steps, pause for students to complete each task. Identify pictures, as necessary.

Building Fluency
Modeling Fluent Reading Select a read-aloud book or a poem that features words beginning with the letter *y*. Read the book or poem several times throughout the week, modeling left to right reading and appropriate expression.

Building Comprehension

Extending Word Knowledge Give students opportunities to talk about new words in different contexts. For example, have students talk about how a **yell** is different from a whisper or a shout.

Understanding Text After a read-aloud, reinforce understanding of the story by asking students to describe what happened in the story. Clarify order of events, as necessary. Ask students who or what the story was about and where the story happened. If the story is informational, ask students what facts they remember.

Writing

To reinforce letter formation, have students practice writing the letter *y* in the following fun way. Using only their index fingers, have students write letters on the floor, then on the desk, the rug, the wall, the table, and the chair. The more texture to the surface the better!

Reinforcement Activities

1. For review, ask students to say the beginning sound that is the same in each set of words. Then have them name the letter that represents that sound.

> *wax, world, winter*
> *light, later, load*
> *nettle, nasty, now*
> *much, mitt, mess*
> *ray, ramp, rabbit*
> *far, foil, fan*

2. Assign pairs of students a letter. Have them search the classroom for objects or pictures of objects that begin with that letter sound. Then have them share their findings with the rest of the class.

Teaching the Letter *v*

Materials: Wall Chart vase, yarn, wagon, goat, and other review objects;
Picture–Letter Cards for *v*
Picture book suggestion: *Ugly Vegetables* by Grace Lin

Quick Review

Ask students to listen and tell you what letter makes the /y/ sound [y]. Then ask them to name the key word for the letter *y* [yarn]. Hold up the Wall Chart **yarn**. Toss the **yarn** to a student as you say /y/. Have the student who catches it say: "*y* says /y/ as in *yarn.*" Throw it a few more times along with other review objects, and have different students respond each time.

Phonemic Awareness

Display the Wall Chart **vase** and ask students to name it. Have the class repeat the word vase several times. Then ask the class to say only the first sound in vase [/v/]. Have them repeat the /v/ sound.

Ask the class what sound they hear at the beginning of *vest*. Is this the same sound as at the beginning of *vase*? Then ask the class to tell you if the following words begin with /v/: *wet, vacuum, run, tube, van, very, window, vegetable, vault, suit, view.*

Phonics

Introduce the Skill Say the word *vase*, emphasizing the initial consonant sound. Ask students if they can name the letter that stands for the sound /v/ that they hear at the beginning of *vase, vacuum,* and *vegetable*.

Write the letter *v* on the board or show the *v* picture–letter card. Tell the class that this is the letter *v*, and it stands for the sound at the beginning of *vase*. Hold up the Wall Chart **vase** or vase picture card. Say the letter name, the sound, and key word: "*v* says /v/ as in *vase*." Then have the class repeat the phrase.

Ask students to name other words that begin like *vase*, then ask what letter the words begin with. Clarify any incorrect responses.

Vocabulary

Introduce New Vocabulary Words from this lesson include **vest, vase, violin, vegetables, vine,** and **valentine**. Clarify the meaning of these words, as necessary, during the lesson.

Completing Student Pages 63–72

Page 63. Read the directions aloud and assist students, as necessary.

Page 64. Model formation of the letter *v* for the class. Have students write the letter in the air as you write it on the board. Have students look at the letter *v* in the middle of the page. Then have them find the number 1 and place their index fingers on it. Ask students to trace the letter, beginning at number 1 and following the stroke of the line. Have students say the letter and its sound as they trace it. Point out the capital letter *V* in the bottom corner of the page. Remind students that capital letters are two spaces tall and are used to begin names and sentences. Reinforce letter formation with the writing suggestions provided for this lesson or by having students practice writing the letter on lined paper.

Page 65. Read the directions aloud and assist students, as necessary.

Page 66. Have the class point to each picture on page 67 as you name it: **vase, vegetables, valentine, vines, violin, vest.** Pause between each word, allowing students time to respond. Then read the questions below and have them follow the directions for the pictures on page 67.

1. I am thinking of a greeting card with hearts and flowers on it. We send this kind of card to people we like on a special day in February. What do we call this card? [valentine] Put your finger on the **valentine**. What sound does **valentine** begin with? Carefully color the **valentine**.

2. I am thinking of a musical instrument you hold under your chin and play with a bow. It is made of wood. What is it called? [violin] Put your finger on the **violin**. Say the sound at the beginning of **violin**. Draw a circle around the **violin**.

3. I am thinking of something you put flowers in. Then you fill it with water. What is it? [vase] Put your finger on the **vase**. Say the sound at the beginning of **vase**. Color the **vase** blue.

4. This is a kind of clothing that has no sleeves. People wear it over a blouse or shirt. Find the picture of it. What is it called? [vest] Put your finger on the **vest**. What sound does **vest** begin with? Draw arms coming out of the **vest**.

5. I am thinking of a kind of plant. As it grows it climbs up the sides of buildings or trees. It has green leaves on it. Its name rhymes with *line*. What is it called? [vine] Put your finger on the **vine**. What sound does **vine** begin with? Draw a box around the **vines**.

6. The last picture shows some things that you might grow in a garden. They are good to eat and make you healthy. You can cook some of them, eat some of them raw, or put them in a salad. What are these things called? [vegetables] Put your finger on the **vegetables**. What sound does **vegetable** begin with? Color the **vegetables** green.

Page 67. Read the directions aloud on page 66 while students listen and work.

Page 68. Read the directions aloud and assist students, as necessary.

Page 69. Read the directions aloud, pausing for students to complete each part. Give praise for slow, careful work.

Page 70–72. Read the directions aloud and assist students, as necessary. If the directions have multiple steps, pause for students to complete each task. Identify pictures, as necessary.

Building Fluency

Modeling Fluent Reading Select a read-aloud book or a poem that features words beginning with the letter *v*. Read the book or poem several times throughout the week, modeling left to right reading and appropriate expression.

Building Comprehension

Using Language Review any new words from the lesson or read-aloud. Ask volunteers to use one of the new words in a sentence.

Prediction As you read aloud to the class, pause at various points throughout the story to ask students what they think will happen next. Confirm correct predictions as you read the rest of the story.

Writing

To reinforce letter formation, have students practice writing the letter *v* in the following fun way. Put a small amount of shaving cream on a tray or other flat surface, and have students write letters in it with their fingers.

Reinforcement Activities

1. Provide students with several picture cards of objects beginning with the sounds/letters learned thus far. Have students sort pictures according to their beginning sounds and/or letters. Then have the students check for accuracy by naming the pictures in each group.

2. Tell students to listen to the words you say and raise their hands when they hear the /v/ sound at the **end** of a word: *five, heat, move, tire, pave, leave, hammer, sound, weave, save.*

Teaching the Letter z

Materials: Wall Chart zebra, vase, yarn, wagon, and other review objects;
Picture–Letter Cards for z
Picture book suggestion: *What if the Zebras Lost their Stripes?*
by John Reitano, William Haines (illus.)

Quick Review

Display the Wall Chart **vase**. Ask students to name it then say the first sound [/v/]. Ask students what letter makes this sound. Toss the **vase** to a student as you say /v/. Have the student who catches it say: "*v* says /v/ as in *vase*." Throw it a few more times along with other review objects, and have different students respond each time.

Phonemic Awareness

Display the Wall Chart **zebra** and ask students to name it. Have the class repeat the word *zebra* several times. Then ask the class to say only the first sound in zebra [/z/]. Have students repeat the /z/ sound.

Ask the class what sound they hear at the beginning of *zoo*. Is this the same sound as at the beginning of *zebra*? Then ask the class to tell you if the following words begin with /z/: *zipper, ladder, zap, sock, mouse, Zelma, sand.* (Be sure to pronounce clearly the difference between the /s/ and /z/ sounds.)

Phonics

Introduce the Skill Say the word *zebra*, emphasizing the initial consonant sound. Ask students if they can name the letter that stands for the sound /z/ that you hear at the beginning of *zebra, zoo, zap,* and *zipper*.

Write the letter *z* on the board or show the *z* picture–letter card. Tell the class that this is the letter *z*, and it stands for the sound at the beginning of *zebra*. Hold up the Wall Chart **zebra** or zebra picture card. Say the letter name, the sound, and key word: "*z* says /z/ as in *zebra*." Then have the class repeat the phrase.

Ask students to name other words that begin like *zebra*, and then ask what letter the words begin with. Clarify any incorrect responses.

Vocabulary

Introduce New Vocabulary Words from this lesson include **zebra, zipper, zoo,** and **zig-zag.** Clarify the meaning of these words, as necessary, during the lesson.

Completing Student Pages 73–82

Page 73. Model formation of the letter *z* for the class. Have students write the letter in the air as you write it on the board. Have students look at the letter *z* in the middle of the page. Then have them find the number 1 and place their index fingers on it. Ask students to start tracing the letter, beginning at number 1 and following the stroke of the first line. To continue, have them find the number 2 and follow that line. They should say the letter and its sound as they trace it. Point out the capital letter *Z* in the bottom corner of the page. Remind students that capital letters are two spaces tall and are used to begin names and sentences. Reinforce letter formation with the writing suggestions provided for this lesson or by having students practice writing the letter on lined paper.

Page 74. Read the directions aloud and have students complete the page.

Page 75. Read the directions aloud. Make sure students are tracking from left to right for each row. Point out to students that the bottom line shows capital letters.

Page 76. Have the class point to each picture on page 77 as you name it: **zebra, zoo, zigzag, zipper.** Pause between each word, allowing students time to respond. Then read the questions below and have them follow the directions for the pictures on page 77.

1. Find a picture of an animal that looks like a horse with black and white stripes. You might see one at a zoo. What is it? [zebra] Put your finger on the **zebra.** What sound does **zebra** begin with? Draw a circle around the **zebra.**

2. I am thinking of a design that goes back and forth across the page. It is called a **zigzag.** Put your finger on it. Say the sound at the beginning of **zigzag.** Draw another **zigzag** next to this one.

3. I am thinking of a place where wild animals are kept safely so that we can see them. What is this place called? [zoo] Put your finger on the **zoo.** Say the sound at the beginning of **zoo.** Draw a box around the **zoo.**

4. The last picture shows something that we use to close up or fasten clothing. It pulls along a little track. What is its name? [zipper] Put your finger on the **zipper.** What sound does **zipper** begin with? Draw a girl's head and arms and legs in the dress with the **zipper.**

Page 77. Read the directions aloud on page 76 while students listen and work.

Page 78. Read the directions aloud and assist students, as necessary.

Page 79. Read the directions aloud, pausing for students to complete each part. Give praise for slow, careful work.

Page 80–82. Read the directions aloud and assist students, as necessary. If the directions have multiple steps, pause for students to complete each task. Identify pictures, as necessary.

Building Fluency

Modeling Fluent Reading Select a read-aloud book or a poem that features words beginning with the letter *z*. Read the book or poem several times throughout the week, modeling left to right reading and appropriate expression.

Building Comprehension

Extending Word Knowledge Give students opportunities to talk about new words in different contexts. For example, have students talk about what they might see at a **zoo.**

Understanding Text After a read-aloud, reinforce understanding of the story by asking students to describe what happened in the story. Clarify order of events, as necessary. Ask students who or what the story was about and where the story happened. If the story is informational, ask students what facts they remember.

Writing

To reinforce letter formation, have students practice writing the letter *z* in the following fun way. Bring in a straw mat, a small rag rug, or a piece of screening, and have students write letters on it with their index fingers.

Reinforcement Activities

1. Ask students to tell you if they hear the /z/ sound at the **beginning** or **end** of each word you say. Use the following examples: *fuzz, zone, zipper, buzz, zoom, size, whiz, zero, zap, doze, breeze.* As necessary, stretch out the individual sounds in each word as you say it.

2. Say a word, such as *Sunday.* As a volunteer to come to the board and write the letter they hear at the beginning of this word. Ask the class to indicate their agreement with thumbs up or thumbs down. Continue saying words until everyone has had a turn.

Teaching the Letter *q*

Materials: Wall Chart **quilt, zebra, vase, yarn,** and other review objects;
Picture–Letter Cards for *q, z, v, y, w, g, l,* and *c*
Picture book suggestion: *The Keeping Quilt* by Patricia Polacco

Quick Review

Display the letter *z*. Ask students to name it and tell what sound it makes [/z/]. Then ask them to name the key word that starts with the sound /z/ [*zebra*]. Hold up the Wall Chart **zebra** and have the class repeat: "*z* says /z/ as in *zebra.*" Continue with *v, y,* and other review letters until all students have had a turn.

Phonemic Awareness

Display the Wall Chart **quilt** and ask students to name it. Have the class repeat the word *quilt* several times. Then ask the class to say the first sounds they hear in *quilt* [/kw/]. Have students repeat the /kw/ sound.

   Ask the class what sound they hear at the beginning of *quack*. Is this the same sound as in *quilt*? Then ask the class to tell you if the following words begin with /kw/: *quote, bite, quit, goat, not, quick.*

Phonics

Introduce the Skill Say the word *quilt,* emphasizing the initial consonant sounds /kw/. Ask students if they can name the letter that stands for the sound /kw/ that they hear at the beginning of *quilt, quack, quick, quote,* and *queen.*

Write the letter *q* on the board or show the *q* picture–letter card. Tell the class that this is the letter *q,* and it stands for the /kw/ sound at the beginning of quilt. Hold up the Wall Chart **quilt** or quilt picture card. Repeat the letter name, the sound, and key word: "q says /kw/ as in *quilt.*" Have the class repeat it. (Although students are probably not decoding words at this level, you may choose to explain that the letter *q* is always followed by the letter *u.* Q never shows up in a word without the letter *u* right after it, and the two letters work together to make the /kw/ sound.)

Ask students to name other words that begin with the /kw/ sound like *quilt,* then ask what letter the words begin with. Clarify any incorrect responses.

Vocabulary

Introduce New Vocabulary Words from this lesson include **question mark, quills, queen,** and **quilt.** Clarify the meaning of these words, as necessary, during the lesson.

Completing Student Pages 83–94

Page 83. Model formation of the letter *q* for the class. Have students write the letter in the air as you write it on the board. Have students look at the letter *q* in the middle of the page, and point out how *q* hangs below the line. Then have them find the number 1 and place their index fingers on it. Ask students to start tracing the letter, beginning at number 1 and following the stroke of the first line. To continue, have them find the number 2 and follow that line. They should say the letter and its sound as they trace it. Point out the capital letter *Q* in the bottom corner of the page and remind students that capital letters are used to begin names and sentences. Reinforce letter formation with the writing suggestions provided for this lesson or by having students practice writing the letter on lined paper.

Page 84. Read the directions aloud. Make sure students are tracking from left to right for each row. Point out to students that the bottom line shows capital letters.

Page 85. Read the directions aloud, pausing for students to respond to each part. Give praise for slow, careful work.

Page 86. Have the class point to each picture on page 87 as you name it: **question mark, queen, quilt, quills.** Pause between each word, allowing students time to respond. Then read the questions below and have them follow the directions for the pictures on page 87.

1. I am thinking of something sharp that is all over a porcupine's body. These pointed things help protect the porcupine. What are they called? [quills] Put your finger on the **quills**. Can you hear /kw/ at the beginning of **quills**? Say the sound. Draw a circle around the porcupine with its **quills**.

2. I am thinking of a woman who wears a crown on her head. Sometimes she is the ruler of her country. Sometimes she is the wife of the king. Who is she? [queen] Put your finger on the **queen**. What sound does **queen** begin with? Carefully color the **queen**.

3. I am thinking of something that you might put on your bed to keep you warm. It is different from a blanket. It often has many colors on it. What is it? [quilt] Put your finger on the **quilt**. What sound do you hear at the beginning of **quilt**? Color the **quilt** in this picture.

4. The last picture shows a mark that you use when you write a question. It is called a **question mark**. Put your finger on the **question mark**. Say **question mark** and the sound you hear at the beginning of it. Trace the **question mark** and then draw a box around it.

Page 87. Read the directions aloud on page 86 while students listen and work.

Page 88. Read the directions aloud and assist students, as necessary.

Page 89. Review the letter name *q* and the /kw/ sound. Remind students that the letter *q* hangs below the line. Read the directions aloud, pausing for students to complete each section.

Pages 90–94. Read the directions aloud. If the directions have multiple steps, pause for students to complete each task. Identify pictures, as necessary.

Building Fluency

Modeling Fluent Reading Select a read-aloud book or a poem that features words beginning with the letter *q*. Read the book or poem several times throughout the week, modeling left to right reading and appropriate expression.

Building Comprehension

Using Language Review any new words from the lesson or read-aloud. Ask volunteers to use one of the new words in a sentence.

Prediction As you read aloud to the class, pause at various points throughout the story to ask students what they think will happen next. Confirm correct predictions as you read the rest of the story.

Writing

To reinforce letter formation, have students practice writing the letter *q* in the following fun way. Provide whiteboards for each student and have them write the letter as large as possible with the marker provided. Then have all students display their boards at the same time to show the accuracy of their letters. Repeat with other letters.

Reinforcement Activities

1. Play Pick a Picture. Place the picture cards for *q, z, v, y, w, g, l,* and *c* along the front of the board. Then say a word, such as *zoo,* and call on a student. The student goes to the board and picks out the picture beginning with the same sound as *zoo* [zebra]. Continue with other words until all students have had a turn.

2. Assign pairs of students a letter. Have them search the classroom for objects or pictures of objects that begin with that specific letter sound. Then have them share their findings with the rest of the class.

Teaching the Letter *x*

Materials: Wall Chart **fox, quilt, zebra, vase,** and other review objects
Picture book suggestion: *Hattie and the Fox* by Mem Fox

Quick Review

Display the Wall Chart **quilt**. Ask students to name it and say the first sound [/kw/].
Ask students what letters make this sound. Toss the **quilt** to a student as you say /kw/. Tell the student who catches it to say: "*q* says /kw/ as in *quilt*." Throw it a few more times along with other review objects, and have different students respond each time.

Phonemic Awareness

Display the Wall Chart **fox** and ask students to name it. Have the class repeat the word **fox** several times. Then ask the class to repeat each sound in **fox** [/f/ /o/ /ks/] after you say it. Have students repeat the /ks/ sound in isolation.

   Ask the class what sound they hear at the end of *box.* Is this the same sound they hear at the end of *fox?* Then ask the class to tell you if the following words end with /ks/: *mix, lamp, six, pear, wheel, sax, right, farm, tax.*

Phonics

Introduce the Skill Say the word *fox*, emphasizing the **final** consonant sound. Ask students if they can name the letter that stands for the sound /ks/ at the end of *fox, fix, box, Max,* and *mix.*

Write the letter *x* on the board. Tell the class that this is the letter *x*, and it stands for the sound at the end of *fox*. Hold up the Wall Chart **fox** or a picture of a fox. Say the letter name, the sound, and key word: "*x* says /ks/ as in *fox.*" Then have the class repeat the phrase.

Ask students to name other words that end like *fox*, and then ask what letter the words end with. Clarify any incorrect responses.

Vocabulary

Introduce New Vocabulary Words from this lesson include **fix, six, box, fox,** and **mix.** Clarify the meaning of these words, as necessary, during the lesson.

Completing Student Pages 95–104

Page 95. Model formation of the letter *x* for the class. Have students write the letter in the air as you write it on the board. Have students look at the letter *x* in the middle of the page. Then have them find the number 1 and place their index fingers on it. Ask students to start tracing the letter, beginning at number 1 and following the stroke of the first line. To continue, have them find the number 2 and follow that line. They should say the letter and its sound as they trace it. Point out the capital letter *X* in the bottom corner of the page. Remind students that capital letters are two spaces tall and are used to begin names and sentences. Reinforce letter formation with the writing suggestions provided for this lesson or by having students practice writing the letter on lined paper.

Page 96. Have the class point to each picture on page 97 as you name it: **box, six, mix, fox, fix.** Pause between each word, allowing students time to respond. Then read the questions below and have them follow the directions for the pictures on page 97.

1. This time, listen for the sound that comes at the *end* of a word. *X* sounds like /ks/ and usually is heard at the end of the word. Say the sound the *x* makes. You can hear /ks/ at the end of a word that means a container or a carton. It is used to pack things in. What is it? [box] Put your finger on the **box**. Circle the picture of this word. What sound do you hear at the end of **box**?

2. Now I am thinking of an animal that is the size of a small dog, is red, and has a bushy tail. Say the name of the animal [fox]. Put your finger on the **fox**. Do you hear the /ks/ at the end? Color the **fox** red.

3. When you are cooking or baking, you put things in a bowl and stir. What do we call it when we stir to combine things? [mix] Can you find the picture of **mix**? Put your finger on it. Put a box around the picture. What sound do you hear at the end of **mix**?

4. If something is broken, then we must repair it or have someone _____ it [fix]. Put your finger on the picture of **fix**. What sound do you hear at the end of **fix**? Find the picture of **fix**, and color it any way you like.

5. I am thinking of a number. It is the number of fingers on one hand plus one more finger. How many is that? [six] Put your finger on the **six**. Say the sound you hear at the end of **six**. Draw a fence around the number **six**.

Page 97. Read the directions aloud on page 96 while students listen and work.

Page 98. Read the directions aloud and assist students, as necessary.

Page 99–104. Read the directions aloud. Remind students to listen to the sound at the **end** of each word. If the directions have multiple steps, pause for students to complete each task. Help identify pictures, as necessary.

Building Fluency

Modeling Fluent Reading Select a read-aloud book or a poem that features words **ending** with the letter *x*. Read the book or poem several times throughout the week, modeling left to right reading and appropriate expression.

Building Comprehension

Extending Word Knowledge Give students opportunities to talk about new words in different contexts. For example, have students talk about things that people may have to **fix**. Encourage them to think of examples from their own experience.

Understanding Text After a read-aloud, reinforce understanding of the story by asking students to describe what happened in the story. Clarify order of events, as necessary. Ask students who or what the story was about and where the story happened. If the story is informational, ask students what facts they remember.

Writing

To reinforce letter formation, have students practice writing the letter *x* in the following fun way. Have the class draw very large letter forms in the air using their fingers as a pencil.

Reinforcement Activities

1. Review all initial consonants from Books A–C. Say a sound [/t/, for example] and ask a volunteer to name the letter that makes that sound [*t*]. Then ask the volunteer to say two words that begin with that sound [*tickle, toad*].

2. Say another sound [/b/, for example]. Then ask a volunteer if they hear that sound at the beginning or the end of the word you say [*rib;* at the end]. Continue with other consonant sounds that often show up at the beginning or end of words, like the regular sounds of *f, d, g, t, m, n, p,* and *l*.

REVIEW SECTION, Books A–C
Materials: All Wall Chart objects

Review

Use all objects from the Wall Chart. Toss an object to a student as you say the initial consonant sound. Have the student respond with the letter name, sound, and key word: "*b* says /b/ as in *bell*," for example. Continue with all objects until everyone has had a turn.

Completing Student Pages 105–110

These pages provide additional review of **initial** consonant sounds presented in Books A, B, and C. Read the directions aloud. If the directions have multiple steps, pause for students to complete each task.

Reinforcement Activities

Continue to play some of the games described in the *Explode The Code* Wall Chart Activity Book. Playing short games at different times of the day helps reinforce learning and make it fun. This resource describes thirty-five different games that can be played using the Wall Chart objects.